ISBN 0-8373-0021-5

C-21   CAREER EXAMINATION SERIES

This is your
PASSBOOK® for...

D1768988

Assistant Accountant

Test Preparation Study Guide

Questions & Answers

NATIONAL LEARNING CORPORATION

EAST NORTHPORT PUBLIC LIBRARY

Copyright © 2011 by

National Learning Corporation

212 Michael Drive, Syosset, New York 11791

All rights reserved, including the right of reproduction in whole or in part, in any form or by any means, electronic or mechanical, including photocopying, recording, or by any information storage and retrieval system, without permission in writing from the Publisher.

(516) 921-8888
(800) 645-6337
FAX: (516) 921-8743
www.passbooks.com
sales @ passbooks.com
info @ passbooks.com

PRINTED IN THE UNITED STATES OF AMERICA

PASSBOOK®

NOTICE

This book is SOLELY intended for, is sold ONLY to, and its use is RESTRICTED to *individual*, bona fide applicants or candidates who qualify by virtue of having seriously filed applications for appropriate license, certificate, professional and/or promotional advancement, higher school matriculation, scholarship, or other legitimate requirements of educational and/or governmental authorities.

This book is NOT intended for use, class instruction, tutoring, training, duplication, copying, reprinting, excerption, or adaptation, etc., by:

(1) Other publishers

(2) Proprietors and/or Instructors of "Coaching" and/or Preparatory Courses

(3) Personnel and/or Training Divisions of commercial, industrial, and governmental organizations

(4) Schools, colleges, or universities and/or their departments and staffs, including teachers and other personnel

(5) Testing Agencies or Bureaus

(6) Study groups which seek by the purchase of a single volume to copy and/or duplicate and/or adapt this material for use by the group as a whole without having purchased individual volumes for each of the members of the group

(7) Et al.

Such persons would be in violation of appropriate Federal and State statutes.

PROVISION OF LICENSING AGREEMENTS. — Recognized educational commercial, industrial, and governmental institutions and organizations, and others legitimately engaged in educational pursuits, including training, testing, and measurement activities, may address a request for a licensing agreement to the copyright owners, who will determine whether, and under what conditions, including fees and charges, the materials in this book may be used by them. In other words, a licensing facility exists for the legitimate use of the material in this book on other than an individual basis. However, it is asseverated and affirmed here that the material in this book *CANNOT* be used without the receipt of the express permission of such a licensing agreement from the Publishers.

NATIONAL LEARNING CORPORATION
212 Michael Drive
Syosset, New York 11791

Inquiries re licensing agreements should be addressed to:
The President
National Learning Corporation
212 Michael Drive
Syosset, New York 11791

PASSBOOK SERIES®

THE *PASSBOOK SERIES®* has been created to prepare applicants and candidates for the ultimate academic battlefield – the examination room.

At some time in our lives, each and every one of us may be required to take an examination – for validation, matriculation, admission, qualification, registration, certification, or licensure.

Based on the assumption that every applicant or candidate has met the basic formal educational standards, has taken the required number of courses, and read the necessary texts, the *PASSBOOK SERIES®* furnishes the one special preparation which may assure passing with confidence, instead of failing with insecurity. Examination questions – together with answers – are furnished as the basic vehicle for study so that the mysteries of the examination and its compounding difficulties may be eliminated or diminished by a sure method.

This book is meant to help you pass your examination provided that you qualify and are serious in your objective.

The entire field is reviewed through the huge store of content information which is succinctly presented through a provocative and challenging approach – the question-and-answer method.

A climate of success is established by furnishing the correct answers at the end of each test.

You soon learn to recognize types of questions, forms of questions, and patterns of questioning. You may even begin to anticipate expected outcomes.

You perceive that many questions are repeated or adapted so that you can gain acute insights, which may enable you to score many sure points.

You learn how to confront new questions, or types of questions, and to attack them confidently and work out the correct answers.

You note objectives and emphases, and recognize pitfalls and dangers, so that you may make positive educational adjustments.

Moreover, you are kept fully informed in relation to new concepts, methods, practices, and directions in the field.

You discover that you are actually taking the examination all the time: you are preparing for the examination by "taking" an examination, not by reading extraneous and/or supererogatory textbooks.

In short, this PASSBOOK®, used directedly, should be an important factor in helping you to pass your test.

ASSISTANT ACCOUNTANT

DUTIES AND RESPONSIBILITIES

Under close supervision, is trained in and performs beginning level professional work for the purpose of acquiring knowledge, skill and experience in the professional field of accounting for departments or agencies; assists in making field investigations, and in auditing of business firms; performs related tasks.

EXAMPLES OF TYPICAL TASKS

Under close supervision, is trained in and performs the following tasks: assists in maintaining general and special books of accounts according to established account classifications, including cash books, purchase books, financial registers, general ledgers and general journals; posting entries from books of original entry and closing entries; preparing trial balances, bank reconciliations, operating statements and schedules; maintaining records of contracts, appropriations, allocations, authorizations and payments; examining invoices, claims, vouchers, and payrolls and verifying their accuracy by consulting supporting records and data; receiving remittances, making disbursements and issuing appropriate receipts; setting up and maintaining codes for funds and reserves; allocating costs and charges; classifying receipts and expenditures; auditing books of business enterprises and preparing reports.

TESTS

The written test will be of the multiple-choice type. The tests may include questions on accounting and auditing principles and practices; maintenance, examination and review of financial books, records and transactions; financial statements, budgets and supporting documents and schedules; interpretations and understanding of financial written material; relations with clients and others; report writing; and related areas.

PROMOTION OPPORTUNITIES

Employees permanently employed in the title of Assistant Accountant who possess a baccalaureate degree, including or supplemented by 18 credits in accounting, including at least one course each in advanced accounting, auditing, cost accounting, and taxation, will receive an appointment to Accountant at the end of one year of satisfactory service. In addition, employees in the title of Assistant Accountant are accorded promotion opportunities when eligible to the title of Accountant by passing a promotion examination. However, all employees must have served permanently in the title of Assistant Accountant for a total period of not less than one year immediately preceding the date of promotion or advancement.

———

HOW TO TAKE A TEST

I. YOU MUST PASS AN EXAMINATION

A. WHAT EVERY CANDIDATE SHOULD KNOW

Examination applicants often ask us for help in preparing for the written test. What can I study in advance? What kinds of questions will be asked? How will the test be given? How will the papers be graded?

As an applicant for a civil service examination, you may be wondering about some of these things. Our purpose here is to suggest effective methods of advance study and to describe civil service examinations.

Your chances for success on this examination can be increased if you know how to prepare. Those "pre-examination jitters" can be reduced if you know what to expect. You can even experience an adventure in good citizenship if you know why civil service exams are given.

B. WHY ARE CIVIL SERVICE EXAMINATIONS GIVEN?

Civil service examinations are important to you in two ways. As a citizen, you want public jobs filled by employees who know how to do their work. As a job seeker, you want a fair chance to compete for that job on an equal footing with other candidates. The best-known means of accomplishing this two-fold goal is the competitive examination.

Exams are widely publicized throughout the nation. They may be administered for jobs in federal, state, city, municipal, town or village governments or agencies.

Any citizen may apply, with some limitations, such as the age or residence of applicants. Your experience and education may be reviewed to see whether you meet the requirements for the particular examination. When these requirements exist, they are reasonable and applied consistently to all applicants. Thus, a competitive examination may cause you some uneasiness now, but it is your privilege and safeguard.

C. HOW ARE CIVIL SERVICE EXAMS DEVELOPED?

Examinations are carefully written by trained technicians who are specialists in the field known as "psychological measurement," in consultation with recognized authorities in the field of work that the test will cover. These experts recommend the subject matter areas or skills to be tested; only those knowledges or skills important to your success on the job are included. The most reliable books and source materials available are used as references. Together, the experts and technicians judge the difficulty level of the questions.

Test technicians know how to phrase questions so that the problem is clearly stated. Their ethics do not permit "trick" or "catch" questions. Questions may have been tried out on sample groups, or subjected to statistical analysis, to determine their usefulness.

Written tests are often used in combination with performance tests, ratings of training and experience, and oral interviews. All of these measures combine to form the best-known means of finding the right person for the right job.

II. HOW TO PASS THE WRITTEN TEST

A. NATURE OF THE EXAMINATION

To prepare intelligently for civil service examinations, you should know how they differ from school examinations you have taken. In school you were assigned certain definite pages to read or subjects to cover. The examination questions were quite detailed and usually emphasized memory. Civil service exams, on the other hand, try to discover your present ability to perform the duties of a position, plus your potentiality to learn these duties. In other words, a civil service exam attempts to predict how successful you will be. Questions cover such a broad area that they cannot be as minute and detailed as school exam questions.

In the public service similar kinds of work, or positions, are grouped together in one "class." This process is known as *position-classification*. All the positions in a class are paid according to the salary range for that class. One class title covers all of these positions, and they are all tested by the same examination.

B. FOUR BASIC STEPS

1) Study the announcement

How, then, can you know what subjects to study? Our best answer is: "Learn as much as possible about the class of positions for which you've applied." The exam will test the knowledge, skills and abilities needed to do the work.

Your most valuable source of information about the position you want is the official exam announcement. This announcement lists the training and experience qualifications. Check these standards and apply only if you come reasonably close to meeting them.

The brief description of the position in the examination announcement offers some clues to the subjects which will be tested. Think about the job itself. Review the duties in your mind. Can you perform them, or are there some in which you are rusty? Fill in the blank spots in your preparation.

Many jurisdictions preview the written test in the exam announcement by including a section called "Knowledge and Abilities Required," "Scope of the Examination," or some similar heading. Here you will find out specifically what fields will be tested.

2) Review your own background

Once you learn in general what the position is all about, and what you need to know to do the work, ask yourself which subjects you already know fairly well and which need improvement. You may wonder whether to concentrate on improving your strong areas or on building some background in your fields of weakness. When the announcement has specified "some knowledge" or "considerable knowledge," or has used adjectives like "beginning principles of…" or "advanced … methods," you can get a clue as to the number and difficulty of questions to be asked in any given field. More questions, and hence broader coverage, would be included for those subjects which are more important in the work. Now weigh your strengths and weaknesses against the job requirements and prepare accordingly.

3) Determine the level of the position

Another way to tell how intensively you should prepare is to understand the level of the job for which you are applying. Is it the entering level? In other words, is this the position in which beginners in a field of work are hired? Or is it an intermediate or advanced level? Sometimes this is indicated by such words as "Junior" or "Senior" in the class title. Other jurisdictions use Roman numerals to designate the level – Clerk I, Clerk II, for example. The word "Supervisor" sometimes appears in the title. If the level is not indicated by the title, check the description of duties. Will you be working under very close supervision, or will you have responsibility for independent decisions in this work?

4) Choose appropriate study materials

Now that you know the subjects to be examined and the relative amount of each subject to be covered, you can choose suitable study materials. For beginning level jobs, or even advanced ones, if you have a pronounced weakness in some aspect of your training, read a modern, standard textbook in that field. Be sure it is up to date and has general coverage. Such books are normally available at your library, and the librarian will be glad to help you locate one. For entry-level positions, questions of appropriate difficulty are chosen – neither highly advanced questions, nor those too simple. Such questions require careful thought but not advanced training.

If the position for which you are applying is technical or advanced, you will read more advanced, specialized material. If you are already familiar with the basic principles of your field, elementary textbooks would waste your time. Concentrate on advanced textbooks and technical periodicals. Think through the concepts and review difficult problems in your field.

These are all general sources. You can get more ideas on your own initiative, following these leads. For example, training manuals and publications of the government agency which employs workers in your field can be useful, particularly for technical and professional positions. A letter or visit to the government department involved may result in more specific study suggestions, and certainly will provide you with a more definite idea of the exact nature of the position you are seeking.

III. KINDS OF TESTS

Tests are used for purposes other than measuring knowledge and ability to perform specified duties. For some positions, it is equally important to test ability to make adjustments to new situations or to profit from training. In others, basic mental abilities not dependent on information are essential. Questions which test these things may not appear as pertinent to the duties of the position as those which test for knowledge and information. Yet they are often highly important parts of a fair examination. For very general questions, it is almost impossible to help you direct your study efforts. What we can do is to point out some of the more common of these general abilities needed in public service positions and describe some typical questions.

1) General information

Broad, general information has been found useful for predicting job success in some kinds of work. This is tested in a variety of ways, from vocabulary lists to questions about current events. Basic background in some field of work, such as sociology or economics, may be sampled in a group of questions. Often these are principles which have become familiar to most persons through exposure rather than through formal training. It is difficult to advise you how to study for these questions; being alert to the world around you is our best suggestion.

2) Verbal ability

An example of an ability needed in many positions is verbal or language ability. Verbal ability is, in brief, the ability to use and understand words. Vocabulary and grammar tests are typical measures of this ability. Reading comprehension or paragraph interpretation questions are common in many kinds of civil service tests. You are given a paragraph of written material and asked to find its central meaning.

3) Numerical ability

Number skills can be tested by the familiar arithmetic problem, by checking paired lists of numbers to see which are alike and which are different, or by interpreting charts and graphs. In the latter test, a graph may be printed in the test booklet which you are asked to use as the basis for answering questions.

4) Observation

A popular test for law-enforcement positions is the observation test. A picture is shown to you for several minutes, then taken away. Questions about the picture test your ability to observe both details and larger elements.

5) Following directions

In many positions in the public service, the employee must be able to carry out written instructions dependably and accurately. You may be given a chart with several columns, each column listing a variety of information. The questions require you to carry out directions involving the information given in the chart.

6) Skills and aptitudes

Performance tests effectively measure some manual skills and aptitudes. When the skill is one in which you are trained, such as typing or shorthand, you can practice. These tests are often very much like those given in business school or high school courses. For many of the other skills and aptitudes, however, no short-time preparation can be made. Skills and abilities natural to you or that you have developed throughout your lifetime are being tested.

Many of the general questions just described provide all the data needed to answer the questions and ask you to use your reasoning ability to find the answers. Your best preparation for these tests, as well as for tests of facts and ideas, is to be at your physical and mental best. You, no doubt, have your own methods of getting into an exam-taking mood and keeping "in shape." The next section lists some ideas on this subject.

IV. KINDS OF QUESTIONS

Only rarely is the "essay" question, which you answer in narrative form, used in civil service tests. Civil service tests are usually of the short-answer type. Full instructions for answering these questions will be given to you at the examination. But in case this is your first experience with short-answer questions and separate answer sheets, here is what you need to know:

1) Multiple-choice Questions

Most popular of the short-answer questions is the "multiple choice" or "best answer" question. It can be used, for example, to test for factual knowledge, ability to solve problems or judgment in meeting situations found at work.

A multiple-choice question is normally one of three types—

- It can begin with an incomplete statement followed by several possible endings. You are to find the one ending which *best* completes the statement, although some of the others may not be entirely wrong.
- It can also be a complete statement in the form of a question which is answered by choosing one of the statements listed.
- It can be in the form of a problem – again you select the best answer.

Here is an example of a multiple-choice question with a discussion which should give you some clues as to the method for choosing the right answer:

When an employee has a complaint about his assignment, the action which will *best* help him overcome his difficulty is to
- A. discuss his difficulty with his coworkers
- B. take the problem to the head of the organization
- C. take the problem to the person who gave him the assignment
- D. say nothing to anyone about his complaint

In answering this question, you should study each of the choices to find which is best. Consider choice "A" – Certainly an employee may discuss his complaint with fellow employees, but no change or improvement can result, and the complaint remains unresolved. Choice "B" is a poor choice since the head of the organization probably does not know what assignment you have been given, and taking your problem to him is known as "going over the head" of the supervisor. The supervisor, or person who made the assignment, is the person who can clarify it or correct any injustice. Choice "C" is, therefore, correct. To say nothing, as in choice "D," is unwise. Supervisors have and interest in knowing the problems employees are facing, and the employee is seeking a solution to his problem.

2) True/False Questions

The "true/false" or "right/wrong" form of question is sometimes used. Here a complete statement is given. Your job is to decide whether the statement is right or wrong.

SAMPLE: A person-to-person long-distance telephone call costs less than a station-to-station call to the same city.

This statement is wrong, or false, since person-to-person calls are more expensive.

This is not a complete list of all possible question forms, although most of the others are variations of these common types. You will always get complete directions for answering questions. Be sure you understand *how* to mark your answers – ask questions until you do.

V. RECORDING YOUR ANSWERS

For an examination with very few applicants, you may be told to record your answers in the test booklet itself. Separate answer sheets are much more common. If this separate answer sheet is to be scored by machine – and this is often the case – it is highly important that you mark your answers correctly in order to get credit.

An electric scoring machine is often used in civil service offices because of the speed with which papers can be scored. Machine-scored answer sheets must be marked with a pencil, which will be given to you. This pencil has a high graphite content which responds to the electric scoring machine. As a matter of fact, stray dots may register as answers, so do not let your pencil rest on the answer sheet while you are pondering the correct answer. Also, if your pencil lead breaks or is otherwise defective, ask for another.

Since the answer sheet will be dropped in a slot in the scoring machine, be careful not to bend the corners or get the paper crumpled.

The answer sheet normally has five vertical columns of numbers, with 30 numbers to a column. These numbers correspond to the question numbers in your test booklet. After each number, going across the page are four or five pairs of dotted lines. These short dotted lines have small letters or numbers above them. The first two pairs may also have a "T" or "F" above the letters. This indicates that the first two pairs only are to be used if the questions are of the true-false type. If the questions are multiple choice, disregard the "T" and "F" and pay attention only to the small letters or numbers.

Answer your questions in the manner of the sample that follows:

32. The largest city in the United States is
    A. Washington, D.C.
    B. New York City
    C. Chicago
    D. Detroit
    E. San Francisco

1) Choose the answer you think is best. (New York City is the largest, so "B" is correct.)
2) Find the row of dotted lines numbered the same as the question you are answering. (Find row number 32)
3) Find the pair of dotted lines corresponding to the answer. (Find the pair of lines under the mark "B.")
4) Make a solid black mark between the dotted lines.

VI. BEFORE THE TEST

Common sense will help you find procedures to follow to get ready for an examination. Too many of us, however, overlook these sensible measures. Indeed, nervousness and fatigue have been found to be the most serious reasons why applicants fail to do their best on civil service tests. Here is a list of reminders:

- Begin your preparation early – Don't wait until the last minute to go scurrying around for books and materials or to find out what the position is all about.
- Prepare continuously – An hour a night for a week is better than an all-night cram session. This has been definitely established. What is more, a night a

week for a month will return better dividends than crowding your study into a shorter period of time.

- Locate the place of the exam – You have been sent a notice telling you when and where to report for the examination. If the location is in a different town or otherwise unfamiliar to you, it would be well to inquire the best route and learn something about the building.
- Relax the night before the test – Allow your mind to rest. Do not study at all that night. Plan some mild recreation or diversion; then go to bed early and get a good night's sleep.
- Get up early enough to make a leisurely trip to the place for the test – This way unforeseen events, traffic snarls, unfamiliar buildings, etc. will not upset you.
- Dress comfortably – A written test is not a fashion show. You will be known by number and not by name, so wear something comfortable.
- Leave excess paraphernalia at home – Shopping bags and odd bundles will get in your way. You need bring only the items mentioned in the official notice you received; usually everything you need is provided. Do not bring reference books to the exam. They will only confuse those last minutes and be taken away from you when in the test room.
- Arrive somewhat ahead of time – If because of transportation schedules you must get there very early, bring a newspaper or magazine to take your mind off yourself while waiting.
- Locate the examination room – When you have found the proper room, you will be directed to the seat or part of the room where you will sit. Sometimes you are given a sheet of instructions to read while you are waiting. Do not fill out any forms until you are told to do so; just read them and be prepared.
- Relax and prepare to listen to the instructions
- If you have any physical problem that may keep you from doing your best, be sure to tell the test administrator. If you are sick or in poor health, you really cannot do your best on the exam. You can come back and take the test some other time.

VII. AT THE TEST

The day of the test is here and you have the test booklet in your hand. The temptation to get going is very strong. Caution! There is more to success than knowing the right answers. You must know how to identify your papers and understand variations in the type of short-answer question used in this particular examination. Follow these suggestions for maximum results from your efforts:

1) Cooperate with the monitor

The test administrator has a duty to create a situation in which you can be as much at ease as possible. He will give instructions, tell you when to begin, check to see that you are marking your answer sheet correctly, and so on. He is not there to guard you, although he will see that your competitors do not take unfair advantage. He wants to help you do your best.

2) Listen to all instructions

Don't jump the gun! Wait until you understand all directions. In most civil service tests you get more time than you need to answer the questions. So don't be in a hurry.

Read each word of instructions until you clearly understand the meaning. Study the examples, listen to all announcements and follow directions. Ask questions if you do not understand what to do.

3) Identify your papers

Civil service exams are usually identified by number only. You will be assigned a number; you must not put your name on your test papers. Be sure to copy your number correctly. Since more than one exam may be given, copy your exact examination title.

4) Plan your time

Unless you are told that a test is a "speed" or "rate of work" test, speed itself is usually not important. Time enough to answer all the questions will be provided, but this does not mean that you have all day. An overall time limit has been set. Divide the total time (in minutes) by the number of questions to determine the approximate time you have for each question.

5) Do not linger over difficult questions

If you come across a difficult question, mark it with a paper clip (useful to have along) and come back to it when you have been through the booklet. One caution if you do this – be sure to skip a number on your answer sheet as well. Check often to be sure that you have not lost your place and that you are marking in the row numbered the same as the question you are answering.

6) Read the questions

Be sure you know what the question asks! Many capable people are unsuccessful because they failed to *read* the questions correctly.

7) Answer all questions

Unless you have been instructed that a penalty will be deducted for incorrect answers, it is better to guess than to omit a question.

8) Speed tests

It is often better NOT to guess on speed tests. It has been found that on timed tests people are tempted to spend the last few seconds before time is called in marking answers at random – without even reading them – in the hope of picking up a few extra points. To discourage this practice, the instructions may warn you that your score will be "corrected" for guessing. That is, a penalty will be applied. The incorrect answers will be deducted from the correct ones, or some other penalty formula will be used.

9) Review your answers

If you finish before time is called, go back to the questions you guessed or omitted to give them further thought. Review other answers if you have time.

10) Return your test materials

If you are ready to leave before others have finished or time is called, take ALL your materials to the monitor and leave quietly. Never take any test material with you. The monitor can discover whose papers are not complete, and taking a test booklet may be grounds for disqualification.

VIII. EXAMINATION TECHNIQUES

1) Read the general instructions carefully. These are usually printed on the first page of the exam booklet. As a rule, these instructions refer to the timing of the examination; the fact that you should not start work until the signal and must stop work at a signal, etc. If there are any *special* instructions, such as a choice of questions to be answered, make sure that you note this instruction carefully.

2) When you are ready to start work on the examination, that is as soon as the signal has been given, read the instructions to each question booklet, underline any key words or phrases, such as *least, best, outline, describe* and the like. In this way you will tend to answer as requested rather than discover on reviewing your paper that you *listed without describing*, that you selected the *worst* choice rather than the *best* choice, etc.

3) If the examination is of the objective or multiple-choice type – that is, each question will also give a series of possible answers: A, B, C or D, and you are called upon to select the best answer and write the letter next to that answer on your answer paper – it is advisable to start answering each question in turn. There may be anywhere from 50 to 100 such questions in the three or four hours allotted and you can see how much time would be taken if you read through all the questions before beginning to answer any. Furthermore, if you come across a question or group of questions which you know would be difficult to answer, it would undoubtedly affect your handling of all the other questions.

4) If the examination is of the essay type and contains but a few questions, it is a moot point as to whether you should read all the questions before starting to answer any one. Of course, if you are given a choice – say five out of seven and the like – then it is essential to read all the questions so you can eliminate the two that are most difficult. If, however, you are asked to answer all the questions, there may be danger in trying to answer the easiest one first because you may find that you will spend too much time on it. The best technique is to answer the first question, then proceed to the second, etc.

5) Time your answers. Before the exam begins, write down the time it started, then add the time allowed for the examination and write down the time it must be completed, then divide the time available somewhat as follows:
   - If 3-1/2 hours are allowed, that would be 210 minutes. If you have 80 objective-type questions, that would be an average of 2-1/2 minutes per question. Allow yourself no more than 2 minutes per question, or a total of 160 minutes, which will permit about 50 minutes to review.
   - If for the time allotment of 210 minutes there are 7 essay questions to answer, that would average about 30 minutes a question. Give yourself only 25 minutes per question so that you have about 35 minutes to review.

6) The most important instruction is to *read each question* and make sure you know what is wanted. The second most important instruction is to *time yourself properly* so that you answer every question. The third most

important instruction is to *answer every question.* Guess if you have to but include something for each question. Remember that you will receive no credit for a blank and will probably receive some credit if you write something in answer to an essay question. If you guess a letter – say "B" for a multiple-choice question – you may have guessed right. If you leave a blank as an answer to a multiple-choice question, the examiners may respect your feelings but it will not add a point to your score. Some exams may penalize you for wrong answers, so in such cases *only,* you may not want to guess unless you have some basis for your answer.

7) Suggestions
  a. Objective-type questions
      1. Examine the question booklet for proper sequence of pages and questions
      2. Read all instructions carefully
      3. Skip any question which seems too difficult; return to it after all other questions have been answered
      4. Apportion your time properly; do not spend too much time on any single question or group of questions
      5. Note and underline key words – *all, most, fewest, least, best, worst, same, opposite,* etc.
      6. Pay particular attention to negatives
      7. Note unusual option, e.g., unduly long, short, complex, different or similar in content to the body of the question
      8. Observe the use of "hedging" words – *probably, may, most likely,* etc.
      9. Make sure that your answer is put next to the same number as the question
      10. Do not second-guess unless you have good reason to believe the second answer is definitely more correct
      11. Cross out original answer if you decide another answer is more accurate; do not erase until you are ready to hand your paper in
      12. Answer all questions; guess unless instructed otherwise
      13. Leave time for review

  b. Essay questions
      1. Read each question carefully
      2. Determine exactly what is wanted. Underline key words or phrases.
      3. Decide on outline or paragraph answer
      4. Include many different points and elements unless asked to develop any one or two points or elements
      5. Show impartiality by giving pros and cons unless directed to select one side only
      6. Make and write down any assumptions you find necessary to answer the questions
      7. Watch your English, grammar, punctuation and choice of words
      8. Time your answers; don't crowd material

8) Answering the essay question

Most essay questions can be answered by framing the specific response around several key words or ideas. Here are a few such key words or ideas:

M's: manpower, materials, methods, money, management
P's: purpose, program, policy, plan, procedure, practice, problems, pitfalls, personnel, public relations

    a. Six basic steps in handling problems:
        1. Preliminary plan and background development
        2. Collect information, data and facts
        3. Analyze and interpret information, data and facts
        4. Analyze and develop solutions as well as make recommendations
        5. Prepare report and sell recommendations
        6. Install recommendations and follow up effectiveness

    b. Pitfalls to avoid
        1. *Taking things for granted* – A statement of the situation does not necessarily imply that each of the elements is necessarily true; for example, a complaint may be invalid and biased so that all that can be taken for granted is that a complaint has been registered
        2. *Considering only one side of a situation* – Wherever possible, indicate several alternatives and then point out the reasons you selected the best one
        3. *Failing to indicate follow up* – Whenever your answer indicates action on your part, make certain that you will take proper follow-up action to see how successful your recommendations, procedures or actions turn out to be
        4. *Taking too long in answering any single question* – Remember to time your answers properly

IX. AFTER THE TEST

Scoring procedures differ in detail among civil service jurisdictions although the general principles are the same. Whether the papers are hand-scored or graded by machine we have described, they are nearly always graded by number. That is, the person who marks the paper knows only the number – never the name – of the applicant. Not until all the papers have been graded will they be matched with names. If other tests, such as training and experience or oral interview ratings have been given, scores will be combined. Different parts of the examination usually have different weights. For example, the written test might count 60 percent of the final grade, and a rating of training and experience 40 percent. In many jurisdictions, veterans will have a certain number of points added to their grades.

After the final grade has been determined, the names are placed in grade order and an eligible list is established. There are various methods for resolving ties between those who get the same final grade – probably the most common is to place first the name of the person whose application was received first. Job offers are made from the eligible list in the order the names appear on it. You will be notified of your grade and your rank as soon as all these computations have been made. This will be done as rapidly as possible.

People who are found to meet the requirements in the announcement are called "eligibles." Their names are put on a list of eligible candidates. An eligible's chances of getting a job depend on how high he stands on this list and how fast agencies are filling jobs from the list.

When a job is to be filled from a list of eligibles, the agency asks for the names of people on the list of eligibles for that job. When the civil service commission receives this request, it sends to the agency the names of the three people highest on this list. Or, if the job to be filled has specialized requirements, the office sends the agency the names of the top three persons who meet these requirements from the general list.

The appointing officer makes a choice from among the three people whose names were sent to him. If the selected person accepts the appointment, the names of the others are put back on the list to be considered for future openings.

That is the rule in hiring from all kinds of eligible lists, whether they are for typist, carpenter, chemist, or something else. For every vacancy, the appointing officer has his choice of any one of the top three eligibles on the list. This explains why the person whose name is on top of the list sometimes does not get an appointment when some of the persons lower on the list do. If the appointing officer chooses the second or third eligible, the No. 1 eligible does not get a job at once, but stays on the list until he is appointed or the list is terminated.

X. HOW TO PASS THE INTERVIEW TEST

The examination for which you applied requires an oral interview test. You have already taken the written test and you are now being called for the interview test – the final part of the formal examination.

You may think that it is not possible to prepare for an interview test and that there are no procedures to follow during an interview. Our purpose is to point out some things you can do in advance that will help you and some good rules to follow and pitfalls to avoid while you are being interviewed.

What is an interview supposed to test?

The written examination is designed to test the technical knowledge and competence of the candidate; the oral is designed to evaluate intangible qualities, not readily measured otherwise, and to establish a list showing the relative fitness of each candidate – as measured against his competitors – for the position sought. Scoring is not on the basis of "right" and "wrong," but on a sliding scale of values ranging from "not passable" to "outstanding." As a matter of fact, it is possible to achieve a relatively low score without a single "incorrect" answer because of evident weakness in the qualities being measured.

Occasionally, an examination may consist entirely of an oral test – either an individual or a group oral. In such cases, information is sought concerning the technical knowledges and abilities of the candidate, since there has been no written examination for this purpose. More commonly, however, an oral test is used to supplement a written examination.

Who conducts interviews?

The composition of oral boards varies among different jurisdictions. In nearly all, a representative of the personnel department serves as chairman. One of the members of the board may be a representative of the department in which the candidate would work. In some cases, "outside experts" are used, and, frequently, a businessman or some other representative of the general public is asked to serve. Labor and management or other special groups may be represented. The aim is to secure the services of experts in the appropriate field.

However the board is composed, it is a good idea (and not at all improper or unethical) to ascertain in advance of the interview who the members are and what groups they represent. When you are introduced to them, you will have some idea of their backgrounds and interests, and at least you will not stutter and stammer over their names.

What should be done before the interview?

While knowledge about the board members is useful and takes some of the surprise element out of the interview, there is other preparation which is more substantive. It *is* possible to prepare for an oral interview – in several ways:

1) Keep a copy of your application and review it carefully before the interview

This may be the only document before the oral board, and the starting point of the interview. Know what education and experience you have listed there, and the sequence and dates of all of it. Sometimes the board will ask you to review the highlights of your experience for them; you should not have to hem and haw doing it.

2) Study the class specification and the examination announcement

Usually, the oral board has one or both of these to guide them. The qualities, characteristics or knowledges required by the position sought are stated in these documents. They offer valuable clues as to the nature of the oral interview. For example, if the job involves supervisory responsibilities, the announcement will usually indicate that knowledge of modern supervisory methods and the qualifications of the candidate as a supervisor will be tested. If so, you can expect such questions, frequently in the form of a hypothetical situation which you are expected to solve. NEVER go into an oral without knowledge of the duties and responsibilities of the job you seek.

3) Think through each qualification required

Try to visualize the kind of questions you would ask if you were a board member. How well could you answer them? Try especially to appraise your own knowledge and background in each area, *measured against the job sought*, and identify any areas in which you are weak. Be critical and realistic – do not flatter yourself.

4) Do some general reading in areas in which you feel you may be weak

For example, if the job involves supervision and your past experience has NOT, some general reading in supervisory methods and practices, particularly in the field of human relations, might be useful. Do NOT study agency procedures or detailed manuals. The oral board will be testing your understanding and capacity, not your memory.

5) Get a good night's sleep and watch your general health and mental attitude

You will want a clear head at the interview. Take care of a cold or any other minor ailment, and of course, no hangovers.

What should be done on the day of the interview?

Now comes the day of the interview itself. Give yourself plenty of time to get there. Plan to arrive somewhat ahead of the scheduled time, particularly if your appointment is in the fore part of the day. If a previous candidate fails to appear, the board might be ready for you a bit early. By early afternoon an oral board is almost invariably behind schedule if there are many candidates, and you may have to wait.

Take along a book or magazine to read, or your application to review, but leave any extraneous material in the waiting room when you go in for your interview. In any event, relax and compose yourself.

The matter of dress is important. The board is forming impressions about you – from your experience, your manners, your attitude, and your appearance. Give your personal appearance careful attention. Dress your best, but not your flashiest. Choose conservative, appropriate clothing, and be sure it is immaculate. This is a business interview, and your appearance should indicate that you regard it as such. Besides, being well groomed and properly dressed will help boost your confidence.

Sooner or later, someone will call your name and escort you into the interview room. *This is it.* From here on you are on your own. It is too late for any more preparation. But remember, you asked for this opportunity to prove your fitness, and you are here because your request was granted.

What happens when you go in?

The usual sequence of events will be as follows: The clerk (who is often the board stenographer) will introduce you to the chairman of the oral board, who will introduce you to the other members of the board. Acknowledge the introductions before you sit down. Do not be surprised if you find a microphone facing you or a stenotypist sitting by. Oral interviews are usually recorded in the event of an appeal or other review.

Usually the chairman of the board will open the interview by reviewing the highlights of your education and work experience from your application – primarily for the benefit of the other members of the board, as well as to get the material into the record. Do not interrupt or comment unless there is an error or significant misinterpretation; if that is the case, do not hesitate. But do not quibble about insignificant matters. Also, he will usually ask you some question about your education, experience or your present job – partly to get you to start talking and to establish the interviewing "rapport." He may start the actual questioning, or turn it over to one of the other members. Frequently, each member undertakes the questioning on a particular area, one in which he is perhaps most competent, so you can expect each member to participate in the examination. Because time is limited, you may also expect some rather abrupt switches in the direction the questioning takes, so do not be upset by it. Normally, a board member will not pursue a single line of questioning unless he discovers a particular strength or weakness.

After each member has participated, the chairman will usually ask whether any member has any further questions, then will ask you if you have anything you wish to add. Unless you are expecting this question, it may floor you. Worse, it may start you off on an extended, extemporaneous speech. The board is not usually seeking more information. The question is principally to offer you a last opportunity to present further qualifications or to indicate that you have nothing to add. So, if you feel that a significant qualification or characteristic has been overlooked, it is proper to point it out in a sentence or so. Do not compliment the board on the thoroughness of their examination – they have been sketchy, and you know it. If you wish, merely say, "No thank you, I have nothing further to add." This is a point where you can "talk yourself out" of a good impression or fail to present an important bit of information. Remember, *you close the interview yourself.*

The chairman will then say, "That is all, Mr. _____, thank you." Do not be startled; the interview is over, and quicker than you think. Thank him, gather your belongings and take your leave. Save your sigh of relief for the other side of the door.

How to put your best foot forward

Throughout this entire process, you may feel that the board individually and collectively is trying to pierce your defenses, seek out your hidden weaknesses and embarrass and confuse you. Actually, this is not true. They are obliged to make an appraisal of your qualifications for the job you are seeking, and they want to see you in your best light. Remember, they must interview all candidates and a non-cooperative candidate may become a failure in spite of their best efforts to bring out his qualifications. Here are 15 suggestions that will help you:

1) Be natural – Keep your attitude confident, not cocky

If you are not confident that you can do the job, do not expect the board to be. Do not apologize for your weaknesses, try to bring out your strong points. The board is interested in a positive, not negative, presentation. Cockiness will antagonize any board member and make him wonder if you are covering up a weakness by a false show of strength.

2) Get comfortable, but don't lounge or sprawl

Sit erectly but not stiffly. A careless posture may lead the board to conclude that you are careless in other things, or at least that you are not impressed by the importance of the occasion. Either conclusion is natural, even if incorrect. Do not fuss with your clothing, a pencil or an ashtray. Your hands may occasionally be useful to emphasize a point; do not let them become a point of distraction.

3) Do not wisecrack or make small talk

This is a serious situation, and your attitude should show that you consider it as such. Further, the time of the board is limited – they do not want to waste it, and neither should you.

4) Do not exaggerate your experience or abilities

In the first place, from information in the application or other interviews and sources, the board may know more about you than you think. Secondly, you probably will not get away with it. An experienced board is rather adept at spotting such a situation, so do not take the chance.

5) If you know a board member, do not make a point of it, yet do not hide it

Certainly you are not fooling him, and probably not the other members of the board. Do not try to take advantage of your acquaintanceship – it will probably do you little good.

6) Do not dominate the interview

Let the board do that. They will give you the clues – do not assume that you have to do all the talking. Realize that the board has a number of questions to ask you, and do not try to take up all the interview time by showing off your extensive knowledge of the answer to the first one.

7) Be attentive

You only have 20 minutes or so, and you should keep your attention at its sharpest throughout. When a member is addressing a problem or question to you, give him your undivided attention. Address your reply principally to him, but do not exclude the other board members.

8) Do not interrupt

A board member may be stating a problem for you to analyze. He will ask you a question when the time comes. Let him state the problem, and wait for the question.

9) Make sure you understand the question

Do not try to answer until you are sure what the question is. If it is not clear, restate it in your own words or ask the board member to clarify it for you. However, do not haggle about minor elements.

10) Reply promptly but not hastily

A common entry on oral board rating sheets is "candidate responded readily," or "candidate hesitated in replies." Respond as promptly and quickly as you can, but do not jump to a hasty, ill-considered answer.

11) Do not be peremptory in your answers

A brief answer is proper – but do not fire your answer back. That is a losing game from your point of view. The board member can probably ask questions much faster than you can answer them.

12) Do not try to create the answer you think the board member wants

He is interested in what kind of mind you have and how it works – not in playing games. Furthermore, he can usually spot this practice and will actually grade you down on it.

13) Do not switch sides in your reply merely to agree with a board member

Frequently, a member will take a contrary position merely to draw you out and to see if you are willing and able to defend your point of view. Do not start a debate, yet do not surrender a good position. If a position is worth taking, it is worth defending.

14) Do not be afraid to admit an error in judgment if you are shown to be wrong

The board knows that you are forced to reply without any opportunity for careful consideration. Your answer may be demonstrably wrong. If so, admit it and get on with the interview.

15) Do not dwell at length on your present job

The opening question may relate to your present assignment. Answer the question but do not go into an extended discussion. You are being examined for a *new* job, not your present one. As a matter of fact, try to phrase ALL your answers in terms of the job for which you are being examined.

Basis of Rating

Probably you will forget most of these "do's" and "don'ts" when you walk into the oral interview room. Even remembering them all will not ensure you a passing grade. Perhaps you did not have the qualifications in the first place. But remembering them will help you to put your best foot forward, without treading on the toes of the board members.

Rumor and popular opinion to the contrary notwithstanding, an oral board wants you to make the best appearance possible. They know you are under pressure – but they also want to see how you respond to it as a guide to what your reaction would be under the pressures of the job you seek. They will be influenced by the degree of poise you display, the personal traits you show and the manner in which you respond.

EXAMINATION SECTION

EXAMINATION SECTION
TEST 1

DIRECTIONS: Each question or incomplete statement is followed by several suggested answers or completions. Select the one that BEST answers the question or completes the statement. *PRINT THE LETTER OF THE CORRECT ANSWER IN THE SPACE AT THE RIGHT.*

Questions 1-5.

DIRECTIONS: Questions 1 through 5 are to be answered on the basis of the following information.

Assume that you are working in an agency and that you are requested to verify certain financial data with respect to the various business entities described below. This information is required to verify that tax returns and/or other financial reports submitted to your agency are correct.

In an auditing review of the income statements of several business firms (Companies X, Y, and Z), you find the financial information given below. Based upon the account balances shown, select the correct answer for the statement information requested.

1. Company X   1.___
   Sales $160,000
   Opening inventory $ 70,000
   Purchases $ 80,000
   Purchase returns $ 1,200
   Cost of goods sold $127,000
   The ending inventory based upon the above data is
      A. $21,800   B. $23,000   C. $24,200   D. $33,000

2. Company Y   2.___
   Opening inventory $ 50,000
   Purchases $145,000
   Ending inventory $ 28,500
   Gross profit $ 56,000
   Sales and administrative expenses $ 64,000
   Sales for the period based upon the above data are
      A. $110,500   B. $166,500   C. $222,500   D. $286,500

3. Company Z   3.___
   Sales for the period $200,000
   Net profit   7% of sales
   Purchases $180,000
   Ending inventory $ 70,000
   Gross profit $ 60,000
   Cost of goods sold for Company Z is
      A. $110,000   B. $140,000   C. $180,000   D. $250,000

4. The opening inventory of Company Z would be   4.___
   A. $10,000   B. $20,000   C. $30,000   D. $80,000

5. The operating expenses for Company Z would be   5.___
   A. $10,000   B. $14,000   C. $20,000   D. $46,000

Questions 6-8.

DIRECTIONS: Questions 6 through 8 are to be answered on the basis of the following information, which is taken from the books and records of a business firm.

Sales for the calendar year	$52,000
Based upon FIFO Inventory:	
Goods available for sale	$46,900
Inventory at December 31	$12,700
Based upon LIFO Inventory:	
Goods available for sale	$46,900
Inventory at December 31	$10,400

6. If FIFO Inventory valuation is used, the gross profit   6.___
   will be
   A. $5,100   B. $15,500   C. $17,800   D. $34,200

7. If LIFO Inventory valuation method is used, the gross   7.___
   profit will be
   A. $2,300   B. $15,500   C. $17,800   D. $36,500

8. If LIFO Inventory method is used, compared with the FIFO   8.___
   method, the cost of goods sold will be
   A. more by $2,300   B. less by $2,300
   C. more by $10,400   D. less by $12,700

9. Which one of the following would NOT properly be classi-   9.___
   fied as an asset on the balance sheet of a business firm?
   A. Investment in stock of another firm
   B. Premium cost of a three-year fire insurance policy
   C. Cash surrender value of life insurance on life of
      corporate officer; policy is owned by the company and
      the company is the beneficiary
   D. Amounts owing to employees for services rendered

10. Which one of the following would NOT properly be classi-   10.___
    fied as a current asset?
    A. Travel advances to salespeople
    B. Postage in a postage meter
    C. Cash surrender value of life insurance policy on an
       officer which policy names the corporation as the
       beneficiary
    D. Installment notes receivable due over 18 months in
       accordance with normal trade practice

11. Able, Baker, and Carr formed a partnership. Able contri-   11.___
    buted $10,000; Baker contributed $5,000; and Carr contri-
    buted an automobile with a fair market value of $5,000.
    They have no partnership agreement. The first year, the
    partnership earned $18,000. The partners will share the
    profits as follows: Able, _____; Baker, _____; Carr, _____.
       A. $9,000; $4,500; $4,500
       B. $6,000; $6,000; $6,000
       C. $12,000; $6,000; no share
       D. $8,000; $5,000; $5,000

Questions 12-13.

DIRECTIONS: Questions 12 and 13 are to be answered on the basis
             of the information below.

    The XYZ partnership had the following balance sheet as of
December 31:

Cash	$ 5,000
Other assets	40,000
Total	$45,000
Liabilities	$12,000
X Capital	20,000
Y Capital	10,000
Z Capital	3,000
Total	$45,000

    The partners shared profits equally. They decided to liquidate
the partnership at December 31.

12. If the other assets were sold for $52,000, each partner   12.___
    will be entitled to a final cash distribution of:
    X, _____; Y, _____; Z, _____.
       A. $15,000; $15,000; $15,000
       B. $24,000; $14,000; $7,000
       C. $20,000; $10,000; $3,000
       D. $23,000; $13,000; $6,000

13. If the other assets were sold for $31,000, each partner   13.___
    will be entitled to a final cash distribution of:
    X, _____; Y, _____; Z, _____.
       A. $14,000; $5,000; $5,000
       B. $8,000; $8,000; $8,000
       C. $15,000; $15,000; $15,000
       D. $17,000; $7,000; no cash share

14. Items selling for $40 for which there were 10% selling   14.___
    costs were purchased for inventory at $20 each. Selling
    prices and costs remained steady, but at the date of the
    financial statement the market price had dropped to $16.
    The inventory remaining from the original purchase was
    written down to $16.

Of the following, it is CORRECT to state that the
_____ overstated.
  A. cost of sales of the subsequent year will be
  B. current year's income is
  C. income of the following year will be
  D. closing inventory of the current year is

15. Dividends in arrears on a cumulative preferred stock
should be reported on the balance sheet as
  A. an accrued liability
  B. restricted retained earnings
  C. an explanatory note
  D. a deduction from preferred stock

15.___

16. The effect of recording the payment of a 10% dividend
paid in stock would be to
  A. *increase* the current ratio
  B. *decrease* the amount of working capital
  C. *increase* the total stockholder equity
  D. *decrease* the book value per share of stock outstand-
     ing

16.___

17. The owner of a truck which originally had cost $12,000
but now has a book value of $1,500 was offered $3,000
for it by a used truck dealer. However, the owner traded
it in for a new truck listed at $19,000 and received a
trade-in allowance of $4,000.
The cost basis for the new truck following the Federal
income tax rules properly amounts to
  A. $15,000   B. $16,000   C. $16,500   D. $17,500

17.___

18. In planning for purchases to be made during the next
month, the following information is to be used:
  Budgeted sales for the month   73,000 units
  Inventory at beginning of the month   19,000 units
  Planned inventory at end of the month   14,000 units
From the above information, the amount of units to be
purchased is _____ units.
  A. 40,000   B. 59,000   C. 68,000   D. 78,000

18.___

19. A branch office of a company has the following plan:
  Cash balance at beginning of the month $ 10,000
  Planned cash balance at end of the month $ 15,000
  Expected receipts for the month $180,000
  Expected disbursements for the month $205,000
In order to comply with this plan, the accountant should
recommend that the branch obtain an additional alloca-
tion of
  A. $20,000   B. $25,000   C. $30,000   D. $50,000

19.___

20. A company uses the reserve method of bad debt expense
and sets up a bad debt account at 2% of sales. The
sales were $500,000. The company wrote off $7,500 in
accounts receivable.

20.___

The effect of these entries on net income for the period
is a(n)

A. $2,500 increase
B. $7,500 decrease
C. $8,000 decrease
D. $10,000 decrease

21. The Daled Corporation has applied to their bank for a   21.___
    $50,000 loan which they will need for 90 days. The bank
    grants the loan, which will be discounted at 7% interest
    (use a 360-day year).
    The Daled Corporation will receive credit in their
    account at the bank for

    A. $46,500   B. $49,125   C. $50,000   D. $50,875

Questions 22-25.

DIRECTIONS: Questions 22 through 25 are to be answered on the
               basis of the information below.

Assume that you are reviewing some accounts of a company and
find the following: the Machinery Account and the Accumulated
Depreciation - Machinery Account.

Machinery

Jan. 1, 1994	Machine #1	20,000	July 1, 1995		6,000
Jan. 1, 1995	Machine #2	16,000			
July 1, 1995	Machine #3	12,000			
Jan. 1, 1997	Machine #4	20,000			

Accumulated Depreciation - Machinery

	Dec. 31, 1994	5,000
	Dec. 31, 1995	10,500

Machines are depreciated based upon a four-year life and using
the straight-line method. Assume no salvage values.

On July 1, 1995   Machine #1, purchased on January 1, 1994,
was sold for $6,000 cash. The bookkeeper debited Cash and credited
Machinery for $6,000.

On January 1, 1997, Machine #2 was traded in for a newer model.
The new machine had a list price of $34,000. A trade-in value of
$10,000 was granted. $20,000 was paid in cash, and the bookkeeper
debited Machinery and credited Cash for $20,000. Income tax rules
should have been applied making this entry.

If any errors were made in recording the machine values or
depreciation, you are asked to correct them and determine the
corrected asset values and proper accumulated depreciation.

22. As of December 31, 1994, you determine that these two   22.___
accounts
   A. are correct
   B. are incorrect
   C. overstate asset book values
   D. understate asset book values

23. As of December 31, 1995, you determine that to correct   23.___
the Machinery Account balance you should leave it
   A. unchanged   B. increased by $6,000
   B. decreased by $14,000   D. decreased by $5,500

24. As of December 31, 1995, you determine that, to reflect   24.___
the proper balance, the Accumulated Depreciation -
Machinery account should
   A. remain unchanged   B. be increased by $10,000
   C. be decreased by $10,000   D. be decreased by $5,500

25. After the January 1, 1997 entry, you determine that the   25.___
Machinery Account should properly
   A. remain unchanged
   B. reflect a corrected balance of $52,000
   C. reflect a corrected balance of $40,000
   D. reflect a corrected balance of $56,000

Questions 26-29.

DIRECTIONS: Questions 26 through 29 are to be answered on the
basis of the information below.

Assume that you are assigned to prepare an Audit Report Summary
on the L Company. The L Company uses the accrual method and has an
accounting year ending December 31. The bookkeeper of the company
has made the following errors:

1. A $1,500 collection from a customer was received on
December 29, 1996, but not recorded until the date of
its deposit in the bank, January 4, 1997.
2. A supplier's $1,900 invoice for inventory items received
December 1996 was not recorded until January 1997.
(Inventories at December 31, 1996 and 1997 were stated
correctly, based on physical count.)
3. Depreciation for 1996 was understated by $700.
4. In September 1990, a $350 invoice for office supplies
was charged to the Utilities Expense account. Office
supplies are expensed as purchased.
5. December 31, 1996, sales on account of $2,500 were
recorded in January 1997, although the merchandise had
been shipped and was not in the inventory.

Assume that no other errors have occurred and that no correcting entries have been made. Ignore all income taxes.

26. After correcting the errors reported above, the corrected Net Income for 1996 was   26.___
 A. overstated by $100
 B. understated by $800
 C. understated by $1,800
 D. neither understated nor overstated

27. Working Capital on December 31, 1996 was   27.___
 A. understated by $600
 B. understated by $2,300
 C. understated by $1,200
 D. neither understated nor overstated

28. Total Assets on December 31, 1997 were   28.___
 A. overstated by $1,100
 B. overstated by $1,800
 C. understated by $850
 D. neither understated nor overstated

29. The cash balance was   29.___
 A. correct as stated originally
 B. overstated by $1,500
 C. understated by $2,500
 D. understated by $1,500

30. Currently preferred terminology for statements to be presented limits the use of the term *reserve* to   30.___
 A. an actual liability of a known amount
 B. estimated liabilities
 C. appropriations of retained earnings
 D. valuation (contra) accounts

KEY (CORRECT ANSWERS)

1. A	11. B	21. B
2. C	12. B	22. A
3. B	13. D	23. C
4. C	14. C	24. C
5. D	15. C	25. C
6. C	16. D	26. A
7. B	17. C	27. A
8. A	18. C	28. B
9. D	19. C	29. D
10. C	20. D	30. C

TEST 2

DIRECTIONS: Each question or incomplete statement is followed by several suggested answers or completions. Select the one that BEST answers the question or completes the statement. *PRINT THE LETTER OF THE CORRECT ANSWER IN THE SPACE AT THE RIGHT.*

Questions 1-4.

DIRECTIONS: Questions 1 through 4 are to be answered on the basis of the information below.

Salary expense was listed as a total of $27,600 for the month of June 1997. Withholding taxes were determined to be $7,250 for income taxes and $1,170 for FICA taxes withheld from employees. Payroll deductions for employee pension fund contribution amounted to $2,500.

Assume the employer's FICA tax share is equal to the employees' and that the employer's share of pension costs is double that of the employees and the employer also pays a 3% Unemployment Insurance Tax based upon $20,000 of the wages paid. The employer pays $1,500 for health insurance plans.

1. The amount of cash that must be obtained to meet this net   1.___
   payroll to pay employees is
   A. $16,680   B. $19,180   C. $20,350   D. $27,600

2. The total payroll tax expense for this payroll period is   2.___
   A. $1,170   B. $1,760   C. $2,340   D. $2,940

3. The total liability for withholding and payroll taxes   3.___
   payable is
   A. $2,340   B. $7,250   C. $8,420   D. $10,190

4. The expense of the employer for pension and health care   4.___
   fringe benefits is
   A. $1,500   B. $2,500   C. $5,000   D. $6,500

Questions 5-6.

DIRECTIONS: Questions 5 and 6 are to be answered on the basis of the following.

The Victory Corporation provides an incentive plan whereby its president receives a bonus equal to 10% of the corporate income in excess of $150,000. The bonus is based upon income before income taxes but after calculating the bonus.

5. If the income for the calendar year 1996, before income   5.___
   taxes and before the bonus, were $480,000 and the effective
   tax rate is 40%, the amount of the bonus would be
      A. $15,000   B. $30,000   C. $33,000   D. $48,000

6. The income tax expense for calendar year 1996 would be   6.___
      A. $60,000   B. $132,000   C. $180,000   D. $192,000

Questions 7-8.

DIRECTIONS: Questions 7 and 8 are to be answered on the basis of
            the information below.

A contract has been awarded to the low bidder. This contractor
will then commence construction of a building for the total contract
price of $30,000,000. The expected cost of construction is
$27,510,000. You are given the additional facts:

	1997	1998	1999
Contract Price as above	$30,000,000	$30,000,000	$30,000,000
Actual Cost to Date	9,170,000	13,755,000	27,510,000
Estimated Cost to Complete	18,340,000	13,755,000	---
Estimated Total Cost	$27,510,000	$27,510,000	$27,510,000
Estimated Total Income	2,490,000		
Billings	$ 9,000,000	$ 9,000,000	$ 9,000,000

7. For 1997, the income to be recognized on a percentage of   7.___
   completion basis would be
      A. $830,000   B. $2,490,000
      C. $3,000,000   D. $9,000,000

8. For 1998, the income to be recognized by the contractor   8.___
   on a percentage of completion basis would be
      A. $415,000   B. $424,500   C. $830,000   D. $1,245,000

9. If the city borrows the $9,000,000 to pay the first billing   9.___
   for the contract above at 10% interest for two years, and
   the second $9,000,000 at 7% interest for one year, then the
   interest costs related to this building are approximately
      A. $630,000   B. $1,800,000
      C. $2,430,000   D. $3,000,000

10. The books of the Monmouth Corporation show the following: 10.___

	1996	1995	1994
Average earnings for prior 3 years	$70,000	$75,000	$78,000
Net tangible assets	$40,000	$42,000	$50,000

   If it is expected that 15% would be normal earnings on net
   tangible assets, then the average excess earnings are
      A. $7,120   B. $8,333   C. $9,800   D. $10,800

Questions 11-15.

DIRECTIONS: Questions 11 through 15 are to be answered on the basis of the information below.

    When balance sheets are analyzed, working capital always receives close attention. Adequate working capital enables a company to carry sufficient inventories, meet current debts, take advantage of cash discounts, and extend favorable terms to customers. A company that is deficient in working capital and unable to do these things is in a poor competitive position.

    Below is a Trial Balance as of June 30, 1997, in alphabetical order, of the Worth Corporation.

	DEBITS	CREDITS
Accounts Payable		$ 50,000
Accounts Receivable	$ 40,000	
Accrued Expenses Payable		10,000
Capital Stock		10,000
Cash	20,000	
Depreciation Expense	5,000	
Inventory	60,000	
Plant & Equipment (net)	30,000	
Retained Earnings		20,000
Salary Expense	35,000	
Sales		100,000
	$190,000	$190,000

11. The Worth Corporation's Working Capital, based on the
     data above, is
        A. $50,000   B. $55,000   C. $60,000   D. $65,000

11.___

12. Which one of the following transactions *increases* Working
     Capital?
        A. Collecting outstanding accounts receivable
        B. Borrowing money from the bank based upon a 90-day
           interest-bearing note payable
        C. Paying off a 60-day note payable to the bank
        D. Selling merchandise at a profit

12.___

13. The Worth Corporation's Current Ratio, based on the data
     above, is
        A. 1.7 to 1   B. 2 to 1   C. 2.5 to 1   D. 4 to 3

13.___

14. Which one of the following transactions *decreases* the
     Current Ratio?
        A. Collecting an accounts receivable
        B. Borrowing money from the bank giving a 90-day
           interest-bearing note payable
        C. Paying off a 60-day note payable to the bank
        D. Selling merchandise at a profit

14.___

15. The payment of a current liability, such as Payroll Taxes   15.___
Payable, will
    A. *increase* the Current Ratio but have no effect on the
       Working Capital
    B. *increase* the Working Capital, but have no effect on the
       Current Ratio
    C. *decrease* both the Current Ratio and Working Capital
    D. *increase* both the Current Ratio and Working Capital

16. During the year 1996, the Camp Equipment Co. made sales   16.___
to customers totaling $100,000 that were subject to sales
taxes of $8,000. Net cash collections totaled $92,000.
Discounts of $3,000 were allowed. During the year 1996,
uncollectible accounts in the sum of $2,000 were written
off the books.
The net change in accounts receivable during the year
1996 was
    A. $10,500   B. $11,000   C. $13,000   D. $13,500

17. The Cable Co. received a $6,000, 8%, 60-day note dated   17.___
May 1, 1996 from a customer. On May 16, 1996, the Cable
Co. discounted the note at 6% at the bank. The net
proceeds from the discounting of the note amounted to
    A. $5,954.40   B. $6,034.40   C. $6,064.80   D. $6,080.00

18. In reviewing the customers' accounts in the Accounts   18.___
Receivable ledger for the entire year 1996, the following
errors are discovered:
    1. A sale in the amount of $500 to the J. Brown Co. was
       erroneously posted to the K. Brown Co.
    2. A sales return of $100 from the Gale Co. was debited
       to their account.
    3. A check was received from a customer, M. White and
       Co. in payment of a sale of $500 less 2% discount.
       The check was entered properly in the cash receipts
       book but was posted to the M. White and Co. account
       in the amount of $490.
The difference between the controlling account and its
related accounts receivable schedule amounts to
    A. $90   B. $110   C. $190   D. $210

19. Assume that you are called upon to audit a cash fund.   19.___
You find in the cash drawer postage stamps and I.O.U.'s
signed by employees, totaling together $425. In prepar-
ing a financial report, the $425 should be reported as
    A. petty cash
    B. investments
    C. supplies and receivables
    D. cash

20. On December 31, 1996, before adjustment, Accounts   20.___
Receivable had a debit balance of $60,000 and the
Allowance for Uncollectible Accounts had a debit balance
of $1,000.

If credit losses are estimated at 5% of Accounts Receivable and the estimated method of reporting bad debts is used, then bad debts expense for the year 1996 would be reported as
  A. $1,000   B. $2,000   C. $3,000   D. $4,000

Questions 21-22.

DIRECTIONS: Questions 21 and 22 are to be answered on the basis of the information below.

Accrued salaries payable on $7,500 had not been recorded on December 31, 1995. Office supplies on hand of $2,500 at December 31, 1996 were erroneously treated as expense instead of inventory. Neither of these errors was discovered or corrected.

21.   These two errors would cause the income for 1996 to be   21.___
      A. understated by $5,000   B. overstated by $5,000
      C. understated by $10,000   D. overstated by $10,000

22.   The effect of these errors on the retained earnings at   22.___
      December 31, 1996 would be
      A. understated by $2,500   B. overstated by $2,500
      C. understated by $5,000   D. overstated by $5,000

Questions 23-24.

DIRECTIONS: Questions 23 and 24 are to be answered on the basis of the information below.

Arnold, Berg, and Cole operate a retail store under the trade name of ABC. Their partnership agreement provides for equally sharing profits and losses after salaries of $5,000 to Arnold, $10,000 to Berg, and $15,000 to Cole.

23.   If the net income of the partnership (prior to salaries   23.___
      to partners) is $21,000, then Arnold's share of the
      profits, considering all aspects of the agreement, is
      determined to be
      A. $2,000   B. $3,000   C. $5,000   D. $7,000

24.   The share of the profits that apply to Berg, similarly,   24.___
      is determined to be
      A. $2,000   B. $3,000   C. $5,000   D. $7,000

Questions 25-27.

DIRECTIONS: Questions 25 through 27 are to be answered on the basis of the following information.

The Kay Company currently uses FIFO for inventory valuation. Their records for the year ended June 30, 1997 reflect the following:

July 1, 1996 inventory	100,000 units @ $7.50
Purchases during year	400,000 units @ $8.00
Sales during year	350,000 units @ $15.00
Expenses exclusive of income taxes	$1,290,000
Cash balance on June 30, 1996	$250,000
Income tax rate	45%

Assume the July 1, 1996 inventory will be the LIFO base inventory.

25. If the company should change to the LIFO as of June 30, 1997, then their income before taxes for the year ended June 30, 1997, as compared with the income FIFO method, will be
   A. *increased* by $50,000   B. *decreased* by $50,000
   C. *increased* by $100,000   D. *decreased* by $100,000

25.____

26. Assuming the given tax rate (45%), the use of the LIFO method will result in an approximate tax expense for fiscal 1997 of
   A. $45,000   B. $50,000   C. $72,000   D. $94,500

26.____

27. Assuming the given tax rate (45%), the use of the LIFO inventory method, compared with the FIFO method, will result in a change in the approximate income tax expense for fiscal 1997 as follows:
   A. *increase* of $22,500   B. *decrease* of $22,500
   C. *increase* of $45,000   D. *decrease* of $45,000

27.____

28. An accountant in an agency, in addition to his regular duties, has been assigned to train you, a newly appointed assistant accountant. He is not giving you the training you believe you need in order to perform your duties. Accordingly, the most appropriate first step that you, an assistant accountant, should take in order to secure the needed training is to
   A. register for the appropriate courses at the local college as soon as possible
   B. advise the accountant in a formal memo that his apparent lack of interest in your training is impeding your progress
   C. discuss the matter with the accountant privately and try to discover what seems to be the problem
   D. secure such training informally from more sympathetic accountants in the agency

28.____

29. You, an assistant accountant, have worked very hard and successfully helped complete a difficult audit of a large corporation doing business in the city. Your supervisor gives you a brief nod of approval when you expected a more substantial degree of recognition. You are angry and feel unappreciated.

29.____

Of the following, the most appropriate course of action
for you to take would be to
   A. voice your displeasure to your fellow workers at
      being taken for granted by an unappreciative supervisor
   B. say nothing now and assume that your supervisor's nod
      of approval may be his customary acknowledgement of
      efforts well done
   C. let your supervisor know that he owes you something
      by repeatedly stressing the outstanding job you've
      done
   D. ease off on your work quality and productivity until
      your efforts are finally appreciated

30. You, an assistant accountant, have been assisting in an   30.___
    audit of the books and records of businesses as a member
    of a team. The accountant in charge of your group tells
    you to start preliminary work independently on a new
    audit. This audit is to take place at the offices of the
    business. The business officers have been duly notified
    of the audit date. Upon arrival at their offices, you
    find that their records and files are in disarray and
    that their personnel are antagonistic and uncooperative.
    Of the following, the MOST desirable action for you to
    take is to
       A. advise the business officers that serious conse-
          quences may follow unless immediate cooperation is
          secured
       B. accept whatever may be shown or told you on the
          grounds that it would be unwise to further antagonize
          uncooperative personnel
       C. inform your supervisor of the situation and request
          instructions
       D. leave immediately and return later in the expectation
          of encountering a more cooperative attitude

KEY (CORRECT ANSWERS)

1. A	11. C	21. C
2. B	12. D	22. A
3. D	13. B	23. A
4. D	14. B	24. D
5. B	15. A	25. B
6. C	16. B	26. C
7. A	17. B	27. B
8. A	18. D	28. C
9. C	19. C	29. B
10. B	20. D	30. C

EXAMINATION SECTION
TEST 1

DIRECTIONS: Each question or incomplete statement is followed by several suggested answers or completions. Select the one that BEST answers the question or completes the statement. *PRINT THE LETTER OF THE CORRECT ANSWER IN THE SPACE AT THE RIGHT.*

1.   The independent auditor's PRIMARY objective in reviewing internal control is to provide

    A.   assurance of the client's operational efficiency
    B.   a basis for reliance on the system and determination of the scope of the auditing procedures
    C.   a basis for suggestions for improving the client's accounting system
    D.   evidence of the client's adherence to prescribed managerial policies

1.____

2.   If there is an increase in work-in-process inventory during a period,

    A.   cost of goods sold will be greater than cost of goods manufactured
    B.   cost of goods manufactured will be greater than cost of goods sold
    C.   manufacturing costs (production costs) for the period will be greater than cost of goods manufactured
    D.   manufacturing costs for the period will be less than cost of goods manufactured

2.____

Questions 3-4.

DIRECTIONS: Answer questions 3 and 4 on the basis of the information given below about the Parr Company and the Farr Company.

The Parr Company purchased 800 of the 1,000 outstanding shares of the Farr Company's common stock for $80,000 on January 1, 2004. During 2004, the Farr Company declared dividends of $8,000 and reported earnings for the year of $20,000.

3.   Using the equity method, the investment in Farr Company on the Parr Company's books should show a balance, at December 31, 2004, of

    A. $89,600   B. $86,400   C. $80,000   D. $73,600

3.____

4.   If, instead of using the equity method, the Parr Company uses the cost method, the balance, at December 31, 2004, in the investment account, should be

    A. $96,000   B. $86,400   C. $80,000   D. $73,600

4.____

Questions 5-6.

DIRECTIONS: Answer questions 5 and 6 on the basis of the information given below about the Fame Corporation.

The Fame Corporation has 50,000 shares of $10 par value common stock authorized, issued and outstanding. The 50,000 shares were issued at $12 per share. The retained earnings of the company are $60,000.

5. Assuming that the Fame Corporation reacquired 1,000 of its common shares at $15 per share and the par value method of accounting for treasury stock was used, the result would be that   5.___

    A. stockholders' equity would increase by $15,000
    B. capital in excess of par would decrease by at least $2,000
    C. retained earnings would decrease by $5,000
    D. common stock would decrease by at least $15,000

6. Assuming that the Fame Corporation reissued 1,000 of its common shares at $11 per share and the cost method of accounting for treasury stock was used, the result would be that   6.___

    A. book value per share of common stock would decrease
    B. retained earnings would decrease by $11,000
    C. donated surplus would be credited for $5,500
    D. a gain on reissue of treasury stock account would be charged

7. On January 31, 2004, when the Montana Corporation's stock was selling at $36 per share, its capital accounts were as follows: 7.___

    Capital Stock (par value $20; 100,000 shares issued) $2,000,000
    Premium on Capital Stock   800,000
    Retained Earnings   4,550,000

If the corporation declares a 100% stock dividend and the par value per share remains at $20, the value of the capital stock would

    A. remain the same   B. increase to $5,600,000
    C. increase to $5,000,000   D. decrease

8. In a conventional form of the statement of sources and application of funds, which one of the following would NOT be included?   8.___

    A. Periodic amortization of premium of bonds payable
    B. Machinery, fully depreciated and scrapped
    C. Patents written off
    D. Treasury stock purchased from a stockholder

Questions 9-11.

DIRECTIONS: Answer questions 9 through 11 on the basis of the balance sheet shown below for the Argo, Baron and Schooster partnership.

Cash	$ 20,000
Other assets	180,000
Total	$200,000
Liabilities	$ 50,000
Argo Capital (40%)	37,000
Baron Capital (40%)	65,000
Schooster Capital (20%)	48,000
Total	$200,000

9. If George is to be admitted as a new 1/6 partner without recording goodwill or bonus, George should contribute cash of   9.____

    A. $40,000   B. $36,000   C. $33,333   D. $30,000

10. Assume that Schooster is paid $51,000 by George for his interest in the partnership. Which of the following choices shows the CORRECT revised capital account for each partner?   10.____

    A. Argo $38,500; Baron $66,500; George $51,000
    B. Argo $38,500; Baron $66,500; George $48,000
    C. Argo $37,000; Baron $65,000; George $51,000
    D. Argo $37,000; Baron $65,000; George $48,000

11. Assume that George had not been admitted as a partner but that the partnership was dissolved and liquidated on the basis of the original balance sheet. Non-cash assets with a book value of $90,000 were sold for $50,000 cash. After payment of creditors, all available cash was distributed.
Which of the following choices MOST NEARLY shows what each of the partners would receive?   11.____

    A. Argo $0; Baron $13,333; Schooster $6,667
    B. Argo $0; Baron $3,000; Schooster $17,000
    C. Argo $6,667; Baron $6,667; Schooster $6,666
    D. Argo $8,000; Baron $8,000; Schooster $4,000

12. Which one of the following should be restricted to ONLY one employee in order to assure proper control of assets?   12.____

    A. Access to safe deposit box
    B. Placing orders and maintaining relationship with a principal vendor
    C. Collection of a particular past due account
    D. Custody of the petty cash fund

13. To assure proper internal control, the quantities of materials ordered may be omitted from that copy of the purchase order which is   13.____

    A. sent to the accounting department
    B. retained in the purchasing department
    C. sent to the party requisitioning the material
    D. sent to the receiving department

14. The Amey Corporation has an inventory of raw materials and parts made up of many different items which are of small value individually but of significant total value. A BASIC control requirement in such a situation is that   14.____

    A. perpetual inventory records should be maintained for all items
    B. physical inventories should be taken on a cyclical basis rather than at year end
    C. storekeeping, production and inventory record-keeping functions should be separated
    D. requisitions for materials should be approved by a corporate officer

15. In conducting an audit of plant assets, which of the following accounts MUST be examined in order to ascertain that additions to plant assets have been correctly stated and reflect charges that are properly capitalized?

    A. Accounts Receivable   B. Sales Income
    C. Maintenance and Repairs   D. Investments

15.__

16. Which one of the following is a control procedure that would prevent a vendor's invoice from being paid *twice* (once upon the original invoice and once upon the monthly statement)?

    A. Attaching the receiving report to the disbursement support papers
    B. Prenumbering of disbursement vouchers
    C. Using a limit or reasonable test
    D. Prenumbering of receiving reports

16.__

17. A "cut-off" bank statement is received for the period December 1 to December 10, 2004. Very few of the checks listed on the November 30, 2004 bank reconciliation cleared during the cut-off period. Of the following, the MOST likely reason for this is

    A. kiting
    B. using certified checks rather than ordinary checks
    C. holding the cash disbursement book open after year end
    D. overstating year-end bank balance

17.__

18. "Lapping" is a common type of defalcation. Of the audit techniques listed below, the one MOST effective in the detection of "lapping" is

    A. reconciliation of year-end bank statements
    B. review of duplicate deposit slips
    C. securing confirmations from banks
    D. checking footings in cash journals

18.__

19. Of the following, the MOST common argument against the use of the negative accounts receivable confirmation is that

    A. cost per response is excessively high
    B. statistical sampling techniques cannot be applied to selection of the sample
    C. client's customers may assume that the confirmation is a request for payment
    D. lack of response does not necessarily indicate agreement with the balance

19.__

Questions 20-21.

DIRECTIONS: Answer questions 20 and 21 on the basis of the information in the Payroll Summary given below. This Payroll Summary represents payroll for a monthly period for a particular agency.

PAYROLL SUMMARY

Employee	Total Earnings	FICA	Deductions Withhold. Tax	State Tax	Other	Net Pay
W	450.00	26.00	67.00	18.00	6.00	333.00
X	235.00	14.00	33.00	8.00	2.00	178.00
Y	341.00	20.00	52.00	14.00	5.00	250.00
Z	275.00	16.00	30.00	6.00	2.40	220.60
Totals	1,301.00	76.00	182.00	46.00	15.40	981.60

20. Based on the data given above, the amount of cash that would have to be available to pay the employees on payday is   20.____

     A. $1301.00   B. $981.60   C. $905.60   D. $662.60

21. Based on the data given above, the amount required to be deposited with a governmental depository is   21.____

     A. $334.00   B. $182.00   C. $158.00   D. $76.00

Questions 22-23.

DIRECTIONS: Answer questions 22 and 23 based on the information given below concerning an imprest fund.

     Assume a $1,020 imprest fund for cash expenditures is maintained in your agency. As an audit procedure, the fund is counted and the following information results from that count:

Unreimbursed bills properly authorized	$345.00
Check from employee T. Jones	125.00
Check from Supervisor R. Riggles	250.00
I.O.U. signed by employee J. Sloan	100.00
Cash counted - coins and bills	200.00
TOTAL	$1,020.00

22. A PROPER statement of cash on hand based upon the data shown above should show a balance of   22.____

     A. $1,020   B. $1,000   C. $545   D. $200

23. Based upon the data shown above, the account reflects IMPROPER handling of the fund because   23.____

     A. vouchers are unreimbursed
     B. the cash balance is too low
     C. employees have used it for loans and check-cashing purposes
     D. the unreimbursed bills should not have been authorized

Questions 24-25.

DIRECTIONS: Answer questions 24 and 25 based on the information below.

The following information was taken from the ledgers of the Past Present Corporation: Common stock had been issued for $6,000,000. This represented 400,000 shares of stock at a stated value of $5 per share. Fifty-thousand shares are in the treasury. These 50,000 shares were acquired for $25 per share. The total undistributed net income since the origin of the corporation was $3,750,000 as of December 31, 2004. Ten-thousand of the treasury stock shares were sold in January 2005 for $30 per share.

24. Based only on the information given above, the TOTAL stockholders' equity that should have been shown on the balance sheet as of December 31, 2004 was

    A. $2,000,000   B. $6,000,000
    C. $8,500,000   D. $9,750,000

24.___

25. Based only on the information given above, the Retained Earnings as of December 31, 2005, will be

    A. $2,000,000   B. $3,750,000
    C. $3,800,000   D. $4,050,000

25.___

Questions 26-29.

DIRECTIONS: Answer questions 26 through 29 on the basis of the information given below.

A statement of income for the Dartmouth Corporation for the 2004 fiscal year follows:

Sales	$89,000	
Cost of Goods Sold	20,000	
Gross Margin		$34,000
Expenses		20.000
Net Income before IncomeTaxes		$14,000
Provision for Income Taxes (50%)		7.000
Net Income		$ 7,000

The following errors were discovered relating to the 2004 fiscal year:
- Closing inventory was overstated by $2,100.
- A $3,000 expenditure was capitalized during fiscal year 2004 that should have been listed under Expenses.This was subject to 10% amortization taken for a full year.
- Sales included $3,500 of deposits received from customers for future orders.
- Accrued salaries of $850 were not included in Cost of Goods Sold.
- Interest receivable of $500 was omitted.

Assume that the books were not closed and that you have prepared a corrected income statement. Answer questions 26 through 29 on the basis of your corrected income statement.

26. The gross margin after accounting for adjustments SHOULD BE

    A. $37,500   B. $35,400   C. $31,900   D. $27,550

26.___

27. The adjusted income before income taxes SHOULD BE

    A. $5,350   B. $9,550   C. $15,000   D. $15,850

27.___

28. The adjusted income after provision for a 50% tax rate SHOULD BE

    A. $7,925   B. $7,500   C. $4,500   D. $2,675

28.___

29. After making adjustments, sales to be reported for fiscal year 2004 SHOULD BE

    A. unchanged   B. increased by $3,500
    C. decreased by $3,500   D. reduced by $2,100

29.___

Questions 30-33.

DIRECTIONS: Answer questions 30 through 33 based on the following budget for the Utility
Corporation for 2004:

Sales	$550,000
Cost of goods sold	320,000
Selling expenses	75,000
General expenses	60,000
Net income	95,000

30. If sales are actually 12% above the budget, then ACTUAL sales will be

A. $550,000   B. $562,000   C. $605,000   D. $616,000

30.____

31. If actual costs of goods sold exceed the budget by 10%, then the cost of goods sold will
be

A. $294,400   B. $320,000   C. $345,600   D. $352,000

31.____

32. If selling expenses exceed the budget by 10%, the INCREASE in the selling expenses
will be

A. $750   B. $3,750   C. $7,500   D. $8,333

32.____

33. If general expenses are under budget by 5%, they will amount to

A. $3,000   B. $57,000   C. $60,000   D. $63,000

33.____

Questions 34-35.

DIRECTIONS: Answer questions 34 and 35 on the basis of the following information.

The Yontiff Company began business on January 2, 2004. During the first month, credit
sales totaled $100,000. During February, credit sales totaled $125,000. 70% of credit sales
are paid during the month of sale, and the balance is collected during the following month.

34. During the month of January, cash collections on credit sales totaled

A. $70,000   B. $95,000   C. $100,000   D. $125,000

34.____

35. During the month of February, cash collections on credit sales totaled

A. $70,000   B. $87,500   C. $117,500   D. $125,000

35.____

Questions 36-38.

DIRECTIONS: Answer questions 36 through 38 on the basis of the following information taken
from the balance sheet of the F Corporation.

Common Stock $200 par	$1,400,000
Premium on Common Stock	115,000
Deficit	50,000

36. The number of shares of common stock outstanding is

A. 200   B. 700   C. 7,000   D. 14,000

36.____

37. The total equity is

   A. $50,000   B. $115,000
   C. $1,400,000   D. $1,465,000

37.___

38. The book value per share of stock is, MOST NEARLY,

   A. $160   B. $200   C. $209   D. $312

38.___

Questions 39-40.

DIRECTIONS: Answer questions 39 and 40 based on the following statement.

    You are examining the expense accounts of a contractor and you discover that, although his payroll records show proper deductions from employees, he has never provided for the payroll tax expenses for these employees.

39. As a result of the oversight described in the above statement, the Costs of Construction in Progress as given on the balance sheet will be

   A. understated on the balance sheet
   B. overstated on the balance sheet
   C. unaffected on the balance sheet
   D. omitted from the balance sheet

39.___

40. As a result of the oversight described in the above statement, the balance sheet for the firm will reflect on

   A. overstatement of liabilities
   B. understatement of liabilities
   C. overstatement of assets
   D. understatement of assets

40.___

_____

KEY (CORRECT ANSWERS)

1.	B	11.	D	21.	A	31.	D
2.	C	12.	D	22.	D	32.	C
3.	A	13.	D	23.	C	33.	B
4.	C	14.	C	24.	C	34.	A
5.	B	15.	C	25.	B	35.	C
6.	A	16.	A	26.	D	36.	C
7.	A	17.	C	27.	A	37.	D
8.	B	18.	B	28.	D	38.	C
9.	D	19.	D	29.	C	39.	A
10.	D	20.	B	30.	D	40.	B

_____

TEST 2

DIRECTIONS: Each question or incomplete statement is followed by several suggested
answers or completions. Select the one that BEST answers the question or
completes the statement. *PRINT THE LETTER OF THE CORRECT ANSWER
IN THE SPACE AT THE RIGHT.*

Questions 1-4.

In the audit of the Audell Co. for the calendar year 2004, the accountant noted the following errors:
- An adjusting entry for $10 for interest accrued on a customer's $4,000, 60-day, 6%
  note was not recorded at the end of December 2003. In 2004 the total interest
  received was credited to Interest Income.
- Equipment was leased on December 1, 2003, and rental of $300 was paid in
  advance for the next three months and charged to Rent Expense.
- On November 1, 2003, space was rented at $75 per month. The tenant paid six
  months rent in advance which was credited to Rent Income.
- Salary expenses in the amount of $60 were not recorded at the end of 2003.
- Depreciation in the amount of $80 was not recorded at the end of 2003.
- An error of $200 in addition on the year-end 2003 physical inventory sheets was
  made. The inventory was overstated.

1. The amount of the net adjustment to Net Income for 2003 is   1._____

    A. Credit $430   B. Debit $430
    C. Credit $600   D. Credit $560

2. The net change in asset values at December 31, 2003 is   2._____

    A. Credit $70   B. Debit $70
    C. Debit $110   D. Credit $60

3. The net change in liabilities at December 31, 2003 is   3._____

    A. Debit $360   B. Credit $430
    C. Debit $560   D. Credit $360

4. The net change in Owner's Equity at December 31, 2003 is   4._____

    A. Debit $710   B. Debit $430
    C. Credit $320   D. Credit $710

5. As of October 31, 2004, the Mallory Company's books reflect a balance of $2,104.75 in   5._____
    its account entitled, Cash in Bank. A comparison of the book entries with the bank state-
    ment showed the following:

    - A check in the amount of $76.25 outstanding at the end of September 2004 had not
      been returned.
    - One check, which was returned with the October bank statement, in the amount of
      $247 had been recorded in the October cash book as $274.
    - A total of $139 of checks issued in October had not been returned with the October
      bank statement.
    - A deposit of $65 was returned by the bank because of insufficient funds.

- The bank charged a service charge of $3.25 for the month of October which was not reported on the books until November.
- The bank had credited $247 representing a note collected in the amount of $250 which was not picked up on the books until November.
- A deposit of $305.50 was recorded on the books in October but not on the bank statement.

The balance in the bank as shown on the bank statement at October 31, 2004 is

A. $2,220.25   B. $2,104.75   C. $2,006.25   D. $2,315.25

Questions 6-8.

A company purchased three cars at $3,150 each on April 2, 2003. Depreciation is to be computed on a mileage basis. The estimated mileage to be considered is 50,000 miles, with a trade-in value of $650 for each car.

After having been driven 8,400 miles, car #1 was completely destroyed on November 23, 2003 and not replaced. The insurance company paid $2,500 for the loss.

As of December 31, 2003, of the two remaining cars, car #2 had been driven 10,300 miles and car #3 was driven 11,500 miles.

On July 10, 2004, after having been driven a total of 24,600 miles, car #2 was sold for $1,800.

Car #3, after having been driven a total of 27,800 miles, was traded in on December 28, 2004 for a new car (#4) that had a list price of $3,000. On the purchase of car #4, the dealer allowed a trade-in value of $1,850.

6. The balance in the Allowance for Depreciation account at December 31, 2003 is   6.

    A. $1,850   B. $910   C. $1,090   D. $1,110

7. The depreciation expense for the calendar year 2004 is   7.

    A. $1,530   B. $2,000   C. $2,500   D. $3,000

8. The book value of the new car (car #4), using the income tax method, is   8.

    A. $1,850   B. $3,000   C. $2,500   D. $2,910

Questions 9-10.

The Pneumatic Corp. showed the following balance sheets at December 31, 2003 and December 31, 2004:

	12/31/2003	12/31/2004
Cash	$6,700	$9,000
Accounts Receivable	12,000	11,500
Merchandise Inventory	31,500	32,000
Prepaid Expenses	800	1,000
Equipment	21,000	28,000
	$72,000	$81,500
Accumulated Depreciation	$4,000	$5,500
Accounts Payable	17,500	11,000
Common Stock- $5 per share	10,000	5,000
Premium on Common Stock	40,000	50,000
Retained Earnings	10,500	13,000
	$72,000	$81,500

Additional information - A further examination of the Pneumatic Corp.'s transactions for 2004 showed the following:

- Depreciation on equipment $2,500
- Fully depreciated equipment that cost $1,000 was scrapped, and cost and related accumulated depreciation eliminated.
- Two thousand shares of common stock were sold at $6 per share.
- A cash dividend of $10,000 was paid.

9. A statement of funds provided and applied for the calendar year 2004 would show that net income provided funds in the amount of   9._____

    A. $2,500   B. $9,500   C. $15,000   D. $22,500

10. The funds applied to the acquisition of equipment during the calendar year 2004 amounts to   10._____

    A. $21,000   B. $28,000   C. $1,000   D. $8,000

11. A company's Wage Expense account had a $19,100 debit balance before any adjustment at the end of its December 31, 2004 fiscal year. The company employs five individuals who earn $15 per day and were paid on Friday for the five days ending on Friday, December 26, 2004. All employees worked during the week ending January 2, 2005. The adjusted balance in the Wage Expense account at December 31, 2004 is   11._____

    A. $22,300   B. $19,100   C. $19,250   D. $19,325

Questions 12-13.

The Peach Corp.'s books reflect an account entitled "Allowance for Bad Debts" showing a credit balance of $1,510 as of January 1, 2003.

During 2003, it wrote off $735 of bad debts and increased the allowance for bad debts by an amount equal to 1/4 of 1% of sales of $408,000.

During 2004, it wrote off $605 as bad debts and recorded $50 of a debt that had been previously written off.

An addition to the "Allowance for Bad Debts" was provided based upon 1/4 of 1% on $478,000 of sales.

12. The balance in the "Allowance for Bad Debts" account at December 31, 2004 is   12._____

    A. $2,550   B. $2,435   C. $2,360   D. $2,240

13. The amount of the Bad Debt expense for the calendar year 2004 is   13._____

    A. $1,195   B. $1,405   C. $1,000   D. $1,510

14. The following ratio is based upon the 2004 financial statements of the Chino Corp.:   14._____
    Number of Times Bond Interest Earned:
        $28,000 / $3,000 = 9.33 times
Information relating to the corrections of the income data for 2004 follows:
- Rental payment for December 2004 at $1,200 per month had been recorded in January 2005. No provision had been made for this expense on the 2004 books.

- During 2004, merchandise shipped on consignment and unsold had been recorded as

Debit - Accounts Receivable	$4,000
Credit - Sales	4,000

(Note: The inventory of this merchandise was properly recorded.)

If the described ratio, Number of Times Bond Interest Earned, was recomputed, taking into consideration the corrections listed above and ignoring income tax factors in the calculations, the recomputed Number of Times Bond Interest Earned would be
A. 8.10 times
B. 7.60 times
C. 6.20 times
D. 5.10 times

Questions 15-16.

The Delancey Department Store, Inc. sells merchandise on the installment basis. The selling price of its merchandise is $500 and its cost is $325.

At the end of its fiscal year an examination of its accounts showed the following:

Sales (Installment)	$500,000
Installment Accounts Receivable	280,000
Sales Commissions	15,000
Other Expenses	32,000

15. The net income for the fiscal year, before taxes, using the installment method of reporting income, is 15.___

A. $30,000   B. $20,000   C. $15,000   D. $35,000

16. The balance in the Deferred Income Account at the end of the fiscal year is 16.___

A. $110,000   B. $80,000   C. $76,000   D. $98,000

Questions 17-18.

The Merrimac Company sold 8,800 units of a product at $5 per unit during the calendar year 2004. In addition, it had the following transactions:

	Units	Unit Cost
Inventory - January 1, 2004	1,000	$2.80
Purchases - March	1,000	3.00
June	4,000	3.20
September	3,000	3.30
October	1,000	3.50

17. If we assume that selling and administrative expenses cost $8,800, the Net Income for the calendar year 2004, using the first-in first-out method of costing inventory, is 17.___

A. $8,460   B. $7,360   C. $6,600   D. $4,070

18. If we assume that selling and administrative expenses cost $8,800, the Net Income for the calendar year 2004, using the last-in first-out method of costing inventory, is 18.___

A. $4,550   B. $7,360   C. $6,600   D. $5,000

19. L. Eron and A. Pilott are partners who share income and losses in the ratio of 3:2, respectively. The balance in the Profit and Loss account on December 31, 2004, prior to distribution to the partners, is $20,800. Before distributing any profits to the partnership in the agreed ratio, L. Eron is to be given credit for interest on his loan of $60,000, outstanding for the entire year, at 6% per annum. A. Pilott is to receive a bonus of 10% of the net income over $5,100, after deducting the bonus to himself and the interest to L. Eron. Giving consideration to all the above information, the total amount of net income to be credited to A. Pilott is   19.____

    A. $8,320   B. $2,080   C. $7,540   D. $15,700

Questions 20-21.

    Schneider and Samuels are partners with capital balances on December 31, 2004 of $15,000 and $25,000, respectively. They share profits in a ratio of 2:1.

    Goroff is to be admitted to the partnership. He agrees to be admitted as a partner with a cash investment to give him a one-third interest in the capital and profits of the business. All the parties agree that the good will to be granted to Goroff should be valued at $6,000.

20. The required cash to cover Goroff's investment in a business partnership according to the terms stated is   20.____

    A. $20,000   B. $14,000   C. $6,000   D. $25,000

21. After his cash investment, and all other initial entries, the credit to Goroff's Capital account is   21.____

    A. $20,000   B. $14,000   C. $6,000   D. $25,000

22. The Marlin Corp. sold 7,800 units of its product at $25 per unit and suffered a net loss for its calendar year ending December 31, 2003 of $2,000.
    The fixed expenses amounted to $80,000 and the variable expenses $117,000. The Marlin Corp. believes that by expending $20,000 in an advertising campaign, it could increase its sales, retaining the $25 per unit selling price, to generate a profit.
    Assuming the above facts, the sales revenue for 2003 reflecting the break-even point is   22.____

    A. $195,000   B. $217,000   C. $250,000   D. $300,000

23. The Anide Corp., which keeps its books on the accrual basis, had the following transactions for its calendar year ending December 31, 2004:   23.____
    • April 15, 2004 - Authorized the issuance of $3,000,000 of 5.5%, 20 year bonds, dated May 1, 2004. Interest to be paid November 1 and May 1.
    • June 1, 2004 - Sold the entire issue at $2,964,150 plus accrued interest.
    • November 1, 2004 - Paid the interest due.
    The interest expense for the calendar year ending December 31, 2004 is

    A. $85,000   B. $165,000   C. $110,000   D. $97,300

Questions 24-26.

    The following information was taken from a worksheet that was used in the preparation of the balance sheet and the profit and loss statement of the Hott Company for 2004:

The Balance Sheet Contained	Amount
Travel Expense Unpaid	$995
Legal and Collection Fees - Prepaid in Advance	672
Interest Received in Advance	469

The Profit and Loss Statement Contained	Amount
Travel Expenses	$7,343
Legal and Collection Fees	5,461
Interest Income	3,114

The proper adjusting and closing entries were made on the books of the company by the accountant and the described information was reported on the financial statements. The books are kept on an accrual basis.

On the basis of the above facts, the balance in each of the following accounts in the trial balance, *before adjusting and closing entries were made,* was as follows:

24. Travel Expense Account

    A. $8,338   B. $7,343   C. $6,348   D. $995

24.___

25. Legal and Collection Fees Account

    A. $672   B. $4,789   C. $5,461   D. $6,133

25.___

26. Interest Income Account

    A. $3,583   B. $3,114   C. $2,645   D. $469

26.___

Questions 27-28.

The following is the stockholder's equity section of a corporation:

Preferred Stock (7%, cumulative, non-participating, $100 par value, 5,000 shares issued and outstanding)	$ 500,000
Common Stock ($1.00 par value, 500,000 issued and outstanding)	500,000 1,000,000
Deficit	(40,000) $ 960,000

27. Assuming two years' dividends in arrears on the preferred stock, the book value per share of common stock is

    A. 78¢   B. 80¢   C. 63¢   D. 94¢

27.___

28. Assuming two years' dividends in arrears on the preferred stock, the book value per share of preferred stock is   28.____

    A. $130   B. $114   C. $98   D. $140

Questions 29-30.

Regina Corporation on December 31, 2003 had the following stockholder's equity:

Common Stock ($10 par value, 10,000 shares authorized and outstanding)	$100,000
Retained Earnings	20,000
	$120,000

On December 31, 2003, the Astro Corp. purchased 9,000 shares of the Regina Corporation's outstanding shares, paying $14 per share.

29. The entry to eliminate Astro Corp.'s investment and the Regina Corporation's stock-holder's equity on consolidation would show a debit or credit to an account called "Excess of Cost Over Book Value" of   29.____

    A. Credit $18,000   B. Debit $18,000
    C. Debit $15,000   D. Debit $19,000

30. If the Regina Corporation had earnings for the calendar year 2004 of $10,000 and had paid out $8,000 of these earnings as dividends, and an entry to eliminate the Astro Corp.'s investment and the Regina Corporation's stockholder's equity were made, the minority stockholder's equity would be   30.____

    A. $15,600   B. $10,100   C. $12,200   D. $14,800

KEY (CORRECT ANSWERS)

1.	B	11.	D	21.	A
2.	A	12.	B	22.	C
3.	D	13.	A	23.	D
4.	B	14.	B	24.	C
5.	A	15.	A	25.	D
6.	C	16.	D	26.	A
7.	A	17.	B	27.	A
8.	D	18.	C	28.	B
9.	C	19.	C	29.	B
10.	D	20.	B	30.	C

TEST 3

DIRECTIONS: Each question or incomplete statement is followed by several suggested answers or completions. Select the one that BEST answers the question or completes the statement. *PRINT THE LETTER OF THE CORRECT ANSWER IN THE SPACE AT THE RIGHT.*

1. For the measurement of net income to be as realistic as possible, it is *desirable* that revenue be recognized at the point that   1.__

    A. cash is collected from customers
    B. an order for merchandise or services is received from a customer
    C. a deposit or advance payment is received from a customer
    D. goods are delivered or services are rendered to customers

2. An accounting principle must receive substantial authoritative support to qualify as "generally accepted." Many organizations and agencies have been influential in the development of generally accepted accounting principles, but the MOST influential leadership has come from the   2.__

    A. New York Stock Exchange
    B. American Institute of Certified Public Accountants
    C. Securities and Exchange Commission
    D. American Accounting Association

3. In which one of the following ways does the declaration and payment of a cash dividend affect corporate net income? It   3.__

    A. does not affect net income   B. reduces net income
    C. increases net income   D. capitalizes net income

4. Under which one of the following headings of the corporate balance sheet should the liability for a dividend payable in stock appear?   4.__

    A. Current Liabilities   B. Long Term Liabilities
    C. Stockholders' Equity   D. Current Assets

5. In which one of the following is "Working Capital" MOST likely to be found?   5.__

    A. "Income Statement"
    B. "Analysis of Retained Earnings"
    C. "Computation of Cost of Capital"
    D. "Statement of Funds Provided and Applied"

6. Which of the following procedures is NOT generally mandatory in auditing a merchandising corporation?   6.__

    A. Physical observation of inventory count
    B. Written circularization of accounts receivable
    C. Confirmation of bank balance
    D. Circularization of the stockholders

7. A company purchased office supplies during 2004 in the total amount of $1,400 and charged the entire amount to the asset account. An inventory of supplies taken on December 31, 2004 shows the cost of unused supplies to be $250.
The entry to record this fact, assuming the books have not been closed, involves

    7.____

    A. credit to capital
    C. credit to supplies expense
    B. debit to supplies expense
    D. debit to supplies on hand

8. A corporation's records show $600,000 (credit) in net sales, $200,000 (debit) in year-end accounts receivable, and $2,000 (debit) in Allowance for Bad Debts. The company's aged schedule of accounts receivable indicates a probable future loss from failure to collect year-end receivables in the amount of $6,000.
Of the following, the MOST correct entry to adjust the Allowance for Bad Debts at year-end is

    8.____

    A. $1,000 credit
    C. $8,000 debit
    B. $4,000 credit
    D. $8,000 credit

Questions 9-10.

A company commenced business in 2004 and purchased inventory as follows:

March	100 units @	$5	$ 500
June	300	6	1,800
October	200	7	1,400
November	500	7	3,500
December	100	6	600
TOTAL	1,200		$7,800

**Units sold in 2004 amounted to 900

9. Under the LIFO inventory principle, the value of the remaining inventory is

    9.____

    A. $1,700   B. $1,875   C. $2,145   D. $2,225

10. Under the FIFO inventory principle, the value of the remaining inventory is

    10.____

    A. $1,650   B. $1,875   C. $2,000   D. $2,025

11. When doing a trial balance, assume that, as a result of a single error, the total of the credit balances is greater than the total of the debit balances. Which one of the following single errors could NOT be the cause of this discrepancy?

    11.____

    A. Failure to post a debit
    C. Failure to post a credit
    B. Posting a debit as a credit
    D. Posting a credit twice

Questions 12-13.

A and B are partners with capital balances of $20,000 and $30,000, respectively, at June 30, 2004, who share profits and losses, 40% and 60%, respectively. On July 1, 2004, C is to be admitted into the partnership under the following conditions:
- Partnership assets are to be revalued and increased by $10,000.
- C is to invest $40,000 but be credited for $30,000 while the remaining $10,000 is to be credited to A and B to compensate them for their preexisting goodwill.

12. After C is admitted and the proper entries are made, A's capital account will have a credit balance of   12._

    A. $24,500   B. $28,000   C. $30,200   D. $36,000

13. After the admission of C to the partnership, C's share of profits and losses is agreed upon at 20%. Assuming no other adjustments, the new percentage for profit and loss distribution to A will be   13._

    A. 18%   B. 32%   C. 36%   D. 45%

14. A company reports as income for tax purposes $70,000 and its book income before the provision for income taxes is $100,000. Assuming a 50% tax rate, the *proper tax* expense to be recorded following tax allocation procedures is   14._

    A. $33,000   B. $40,000   C. $50,000   D. $60,000

15. The relationship between the total of cash and current receivables to total current liabilities is *commonly* referred to by accountants as the   15._

    A. acid-test ratio   B. cross-statement ratio
    C. current ratio   D. R.O.I. ratio

16. On a statement of sources and application of funds, the depreciation expense is *normally* shown as a(n)   16._

    A. addition to operating income
    B. subtraction from funds provided
    C. addition to funds applied
    D. reduction from operating income

17. Company A owns 100% of the capital stock of Company B and reports on a consolidated basis. During the year, Company A sold inventory to Company B at a profit of $100,000. One half of this inventory has been sold at year-end by Company B to the public. Which one of the following would be the MOST correct adjustment, if any, to make the consolidated retained earnings conform to generally accepted accounting principles?   17._

    A. Decrease by $50,000   B. Increase by $50,000
    C. Increase by $100,000   D. No adjustment

18. X, Y and Z are partners with capital of $11,000, $12,000 and $4,500. X has a loan due from the partnership to him of $2,000. Profits and losses are shared in the ratio of 4:5:1 respectively. The partnership has paid off all outside liabilities, and its remaining assets consist of $9,000 in cash and $20,500 of accounts receivable. The partners agree to disburse the $9,000 to themselves in such a way that, even if one of the receivables is realized, no partner will have been overpaid.
Under these conditions, which of the following *most nearly* represents the amount to be paid to partner X?   18._

    A. $1,960   B. $3,200   C. $4,800   D. $5,000

19. R Company needs $2,000,000 to finance an expansion of plant facilities. The company   19.____
expects to earn a return of 15% on this investment before considering the cost of capital
or income taxes. The average income tax rate for the R Company is 40%.
If the company raises the funds by issuing 6% bonds at face value, the earnings available to common stockholders after the new plant facilities are in operation may be
expected to increase by

    A. $65,000   B. $70,000   C. $108,000   D. $116,000

20. The budget for a given factory overhead cost was $150,000 for the year. The actual cost   20.____
for the year was $125,000. Based on these facts, it can be said that the plant manager
has done a better job than expected in controlling this cost if the cost is a

    A.   semi-variable cost
    B.   variable cost and actual production was 83-1/3% of budgeted production
    C.   semi-variable cost which includes a fixed element of $25,000 per period
    D.   variable cost and actual production was equal to budgeted production

21. The Home Office account on the books of the City Branch shows a credit balance of   21.____
$15,000 at the end of a year and the City Branch account on the books of the Home
Office shows a debit balance of $12,000.
Of the following, the *most likely* reason for the discrepancy in the two accounts is that

    A.   merchandise shipped by the Home Office to the branch has not been recorded by
        the branch
    B.   the Home Office has not recorded a branch loss for the first quarter of the year
    C.   the branch has just mailed a check for $3,000 to the Home Office which has not yet
        been received by the Home Office
    D.   the Home Office has not yet recorded the branch profit for the first quarter of the
        year

22. The concept of matching costs and revenues means that   22.____

    A.   the expenses offset against revenues should be related to the same time period
    B.   revenues are at least as great as expenses on the average
    C.   revenues and expenses are equal
    D.   net income equals revenues minus expenses for the same earning period

23. If the inventory at the end of the current year is understated, and the error is not caught   23.____
during the following year, the effect is to

    A.   *overstate* the income for the two-year period
    B.   *overstate* income this year and understate income next year
    C.   *understate* income this year and overstate income next year
    D.   *understate* income this year, with no effect on the income of the next year

KEY (CORRECT ANSWERS)

1.	D	11.	C	21.	D
2.	B	12.	B	22.	A
3.	A	13.	B	23.	C
4.	C	14.	C		
5.	D	15.	A		
6.	D	16.	A		
7.	B	17.	A		
8.	D	18.	C		
9.	A	19.	C		
10.	C	20.	D		

EXAMINATION SECTION

TEST 1

DIRECTIONS: Each question or incomplete statement is followed by several suggested answers or completions. Select the one that BEST answers the question or completes the statement. *PRINT THE LETTER OF THE CORRECT ANSWER IN THE SPACE AT THE RIGHT.*

1. A long-term liability of a corporation is represented by   1.___
   A. stock certificates issued
   B. stock subscriptions received
   C. the balance of a sinking fund
   D. bonds issued

2. Which is an advantage of incorporating?   2.___
   A. Establishing good will
   B. Acquiring treasury stock
   C. Limiting the liability of the owners
   D. Avoiding governmental control

3. Undistributed profits of a corporation are shown in the   3.___
   _____ account.
   A. earned surplus   B. treasury stock
   C. capital stock   D. bonds payable

4. The TOTAL amount of equity, or ownership, in a corporation   4.___
   is found by adding
   A. treasury stock and surplus
   B. capital stock and subscriptions
   C. capital stock and surplus
   D. capital stock and good will

5. On January 1, 1988, the earned surplus account of the   5.___
   Kalfur Corporation had a credit balance of $42,300. The
   net income for 1988 (after taxes) was $12,500. The
   dividends declared for 1988 amounted to $8,400.
   The balance of the earned surplus account on December 31,
   1988 after the books were closed was
   A. $4,100   B. $33,900   C. $38,200   D. $46,400

6. The State Disability Benefits Insurance law provides   6.___
   benefits for an employee or his family when the employee
   A. dies
   B. retires
   C. is temporarily unable to work because of an off-the-
      job accident
   D. is temporarily unable to work because of an on-the-
      job accident

7. Which account does NOT belong in the current liability   7.___
   section of a balance sheet?
   _____ payable.
   A. Interest   B. Notes   C. Accounts   D. Mortgage

8. If the merchandise inventory on hand at the end of 1988   8. ____
was overstated, what would be the effect?
   A. Understatement of income for 1988
   B. Overstatement of income for 1988
   C. Understatement of assets at the end of 1988
   D. No effect on income or assets

9. The face value of a 45-day, 6% promissory note is $740.   9. ____
The maturity value of the note will be
   A. $734.45   B. $740.00   C. $745.55   D. $747.40

10. When cash is received as a result of sales, the PROPER   10. ____
business procedure is to
   A. put the cash in the petty cash box
   B. deposit the cash in a checking account at the end of
     the day
   C. deposit the cash in a savings account at the end of
     the day
   D. use the cash to pay current bills

11. Which item can be determined from information on the   11. ____
Income Statement (Profit and Loss Statement)?
   A. Working capital
   B. Rate of merchandise turnover
   C. Total liabilities
   D. Owner's worth

12. Which item belongs on the Income Statement for the year?   12. ____
   A. B. Rand, Drawing
   B. Accrued Salaries, Payable
   C. Purchases Discount
   D. Allowance for Depreciation of Furniture and Fixtures

13. _____ tax is affected by the number of exemptions claimed.   13. ____
   A. FICA
   B. State unemployment insurance
   C. State income tax
   D. Federal unemployment insurance

14. The source of an entry in the Cash Payments Journal is a   14. ____
   A. sales invoice   B. checkbook stub
   C. petty cash voucher   D. general ledger

15. If a partnership agreement does not indicate how profits   15. ____
and losses are to be divided, then they will be distri-
buted
   A. equally
   B. in proportion to investment
   C. according to duties and responsibilities
   D. by a court

16. The two parties on a promissory note are known as the   16. ____
_____ and _____.
   A. drawee; maker   B. drawee; drawer
   C. payee; drawee   D. payee; maker

17. In order to find the correct available cash balance when
    reconciling the checkbook balance with the bank balance,
    outstanding checks should be _____ balance.
    A. added to the checkbook
    B. subtracted from the checkbook
    C. added to the bank
    D. subtracted from the bank

17.___

18. A check drawn by a bank on funds that it has on deposit
    in another bank is known as a
    A. bank draft   B. certified check
    C. cashier's check   D. money order

18.___

19. _____ tax is contributed by the employee and matched by
    the employer.
    A. State unemployment insurance
    B. State income tax
    C. FICA
    D. Federal unemployment insurance

19.___

20. Which general ledger account would appear in a post-
    closing trial balance?
    A. Interest Income   B. Notes Receivable
    C. Sales Discount   D. Bad Debts Expense

20.___

21. A time draft frequently used in connection with a purchase
    of merchandise is a
    A. trade acceptance   B. check
    C. cashier's check   D. bank draft

21.___

22. A list of accounts and their balances prepared from a
    subsidiary ledger is called a
    A. statement of account   B. trial balance
    C. balance sheet   D. schedule

22.___

23. A time draft which states on its face that it resulted
    from the sale or purchase of merchandise is called a
    A. promissory note   B. purchase order
    C. bank draft   D. trade acceptance

23.___

24. A truck is purchased for $14,800. It is estimated that
    the truck will be used for four years. At the end of the
    four years, it is estimated that the truck will have a
    scrap value of $10,900.
    The amount of annual depreciation is
    A. $3,900   B. $1,425   C. $1,200   D. $975

24.___

25. The current ratio is found by
    A. *dividing* current assets by current liabilities
    B. *subtracting* current liabilities from current assets
    C. *subtracting* total liabilities from total assets
    D. *dividing* current assets by net income

25.___

KEY (CORRECT ANSWERS)

1.	D	11.	B
2.	C	12.	C
3.	A	13.	C
4.	C	14.	B
5.	D	15.	A
6.	C	16.	D
7.	D	17.	D
8.	B	18.	A
9.	C	19.	C
10.	B	20.	B

21. A
22. D
23. D
24. D
25. A

TEST 2

DIRECTIONS: Each question or incomplete statement is followed by several suggested answers or completions. Select the one that BEST answers the question or completes the statement. *PRINT THE LETTER OF THE CORRECT ANSWER IN THE SPACE AT THE RIGHT.*

1. The Federal individual income tax return must be filed by   1.___
   A. December 31   B. March 15
   C. April 15   D. June 30

2. When a firm discounts its own note at a bank, the account   2.___
   to be credited is
   A. Cash
   B. Notes Payable
   C. Notes Receivable Discounted
   D. Accounts Payable

3. Brooks and Carton are partners with an investment of   3.___
   $50,000 and $25,000, respectively.
   How much should be credited to Brooks as his share of a
   $60,000 profit if their agreement provides that the
   partners are to share profits and losses in proportion
   to their investments?
   A. $20,000   B. $30,000   C. $40,000   D. $50,000

4. At the end of the month, the total of the Schedule of   4.___
   Accounts Payable should equal the
   A. total of the Purchases column in the Purchases Journal
   B. total of the Accounts Payable column in the Cash
      Payments Journal
   C. balance of the Accounts Payable account in the General
      Ledger
   D. balance of the Purchases account in the General Ledger

5. When depreciation on a fixed asset is recorded, the effect   5.___
   of the entry on the fundamental bookkeeping equation is
   that the
   A. assets and capital remain unchanged
   B. assets increase; capital decreases
   C. assets decrease; capital decreases
   D. assets decrease; capital increases

6. The ORIGINAL source of an entry in the Purchases Journal   6.___
   is a
   A. purchase invoice   B. stock inventory card
   C. purchase order   D. creditor's account

7. The business form which is sent to each customer at the   7.___
   end of the month summarizing the transactions with him
   is called a
   A. schedule   B. statement of account
   C. sales invoice   D. voucher

8. When we receive a bank draft from a customer, our book-   8.____
    keeper should debit
    A. Notes Payable   B. Notes Receivable
    C. Accounts Receivable   D. Cash

9. The gross sales of a business are $170,000 and Sales   9.____
    Returns and Allowances $450. It is estimated that an
    additional allowance of 1% of net sales will be required.
    The amount listed for Bad Debts Expense on the Income
    Statement should be
    A. $1,250   B. $1,695.50   C. $1,700   D. $1,704.50

10. Which group of accounts will appear on a post-closing   10.____
    trial balance?
    A. Assets, liabilities, and expenses
    B. Income and expenses
    C. Liabilities, capital, and income
    D. Assets, liabilities, and capital

Questions 11-16.

DIRECTIONS: Questions 11 through 16 are to be answered SOLELY on the
              basis of the last part of the bank statement below,
              mailed to Arthur Greene for the month of June.

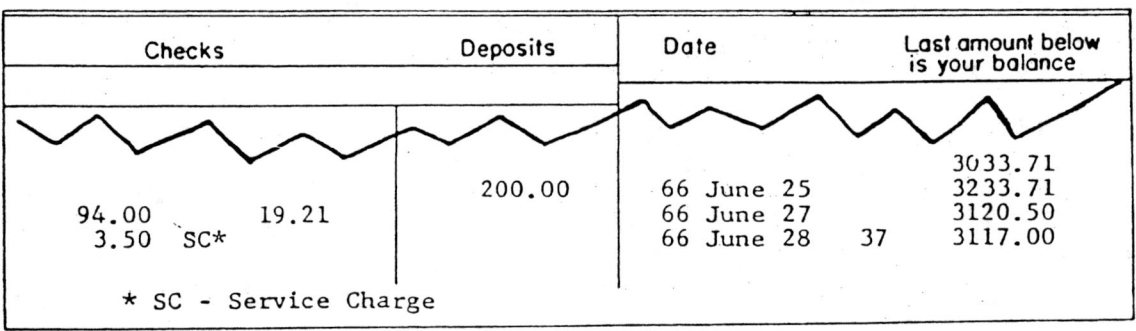

Checks	Deposits	Date	Last amount below is your balance
			3033.71
94.00 19.21	200.00	66 June 25	3233.71
3.50 SC*		66 June 27	3120.50
		66 June 28 37	3117.00
* SC - Service Charge			

All the checks written have been paid except four. The last check
written in June is No. 316. The stubs for the four outstanding
checks are:

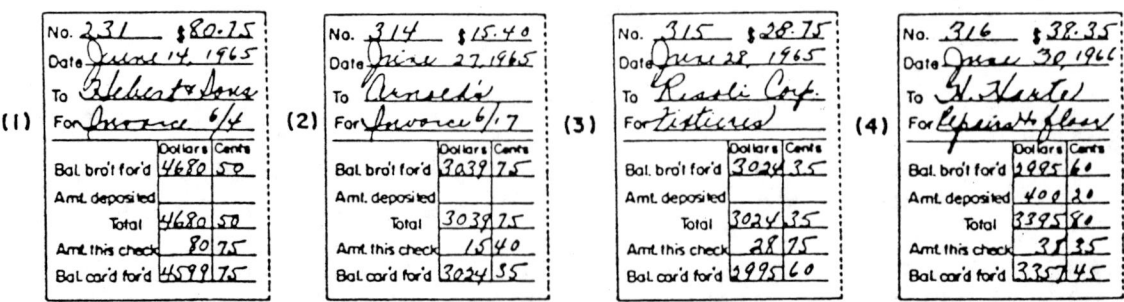

11. From the information available, what was Greene's
    corrected checkbook balance on June 30?   11.___
    A. $3,357.45   B. $3,117.00
    C. $3,353.95   D. $3,120.50

12. Which is the BEST reason that the deposit of $400.20,   12.___
    shown on Stub No. 316, does not appear on the bank
    statement?
    A. The bank has made an error.
    B. The bank has not credited his account.
    C. The withdrawals equal the deposits.
    D. The checks included in the deposit have not cleared
       the banks on which they were written.

13. When he examined the checks returned by his bank, Greene   13.___
    discovered that a check he had written for $44 had been
    incorrectly entered on the stub as $24.
    He should correct this error by
    A. adding $20 to his checkbook balance
    B. notifying his bank to add $20 to his account
    C. subtracting $20 from his checkbook balance
    D. subtracting $24 from his checkbook balance

14. On May 25, Greene wrote and had his bank certify a check   14.___
    for $150, which he mailed to Garcia, the payee. Garcia
    received the check on May 27 and deposited it in his bank
    on June 1. It was presented to Greene's bank and cleared
    for payment on June 2.
    On which date did Greene's bank deduct the $150 from his
    account?
    A. May 25   B. May 27   C. June 1   D. June 2

15. The journal entry to record the bank service charge shown   15.___
    on the bank statement should be made in the
    A. Petty Cashbook   B. General Journal
    C. Cash Receipts Journal   D. Cash Payments Journal

16. Greene's bookkeeper should prepare a bank reconciliation   16.___
    for June MAINLY to determine
    A. possible errors by comparing Greene's checkbook
       balance with the bank balance
    B. the total amount of checks written during the month
    C. which checks are still outstanding
    D. the total amount of cash deposited during the month

17. Which statement concerning a check is MOST accurate?   17.___
    A. A canceled check may be used to prove payment.
    B. Two signatures are required on each check drawn on
       a joint checking account.
    C. The corporation's name should be signed on the
       signature line of a check.
    D. Checks mailed for deposit should be endorsed by means
       of a blank endorsement.

18. If a check which has been certified is not used, which is   18. ___
    the RECOMMENDED business practice?
    A. Mark the check *Void* and add the amount to the check-
       book balance.
    B. Send a *stop payment* order to the bank.
    C. Deposit the check.
    D. Destroy the check.

19. Ames' bank returned a check which he had deposited, marked   19. ___
    N.S.F.
    This notation indicates that the
    A. check has been improperly endorsed
    B. drawer has overdrawn his bank account
    C. drawer has stopped payment on the check
    D. signature on the check has been forged

20. In order to determine the correct available bank balance,   20. ___
    the amount of a deposit made, but not yet recorded in an
    account, should be _____ balance.
    A. *added* to the checkbook
    B. *added* to the bank balance
    C. *subtracted* from the checkbook
    D. *subtracted* from the bank

Questions 21-25.

DIRECTIONS: Questions 21 through 25 are to be answered on the basis
              of the following depreciation record.

DEPRECIATION RECORD			
Delivery Truck Asset	Tractson Make	04387A Number	July 1, 1985 Acquired
$4,000 Cost	5 years Estimated Life	$500 Salvage Value	straight-line Meth. of Depr.

Year	1st quarter	2nd quarter	3rd quarter	4th quarter
1			$175	$175
2	. . .	. . .	$175	$175
3	$175	$175		
4	$175			
5				
6				

21. According to the record, the LAST adjusting entry had been   21. ___
    made on or about
    A. June 1, 1985   B. June 1, 1986
    C. December 31, 1986   D. March 31, 1987

22. The book value on the date of the latest entry is   22.___
    A. $500   B. $2,275   C. $2,775   D. $3,500

23. The TOTAL amount of depreciation which would be recorded   23.___
during the lifetime of the truck is
    A. $4,500   B. $4,000   C. $3,500   D. $500

24. What is the annual rate of depreciation for the truck?   24.___
    A. 17.5%   B. 2%   C. 20%   D. 5%

25. If a business uses the straight-line method of deprecia-   25.___
tion, which is CORRECT?
    A. All assets are depreciated at the same rate.
    B. The older the asset, the greater the amount of
       depreciation recorded each year.
    C. The rate of depreciation is the same each year for
       a particular asset.
    D. The salvage value will be the same for all fixed
       assets.

KEY (CORRECT ANSWERS)

1. C		11. C	
2. B		12. B	
3. C		13. C	
4. C		14. A	
5. C		15. D	
6. A		16. A	
7. B		17. A	
8. D		18. C	
9. B		19. B	
10. D		20. B	

21. D
22. C
23. C
24. A
25. C

TEST 3

DIRECTIONS: Each question or incomplete statement is followed by several suggested answers or completions. Select the one that BEST answers the question or completes the statement. *PRINT THE LETTER OF THE CORRECT ANSWER IN THE SPACE AT THE RIGHT.*

1. Entries in the Cash Payments Journal are USUALLY recorded from
   A. purchase invoices
   B. check stubs
   C. cancelled checks
   D. expense sheets

   1.___

2. A bank draft received from a customer is recorded in the
   A. General Journal
   B. Note Register
   C. Sales Journal
   D. Cash Receipts Journal

   2.___

3. When sales taxes are collected from cash customers, the account credited is
   A. Sales Tax Payable
   B. Sales Tax
   C. Cash
   D. Accounts Payable

   3.___

4. One advantage of the corporate form of business is
   A. limited life
   B. limited capital
   C. limited liability
   D. dissolution on death of an officer

   4.___

5. Current assets minus current liabilities equals
   A. current turnover
   B. current ratio
   C. asset ratio
   D. working capital

   5.___

6. What is the LATEST date that an invoice dated October 15 with terms net 10 E.O.M. should be paid?
   A. October 25
   B. October 31
   C. November 10
   D. November 30

   6.___

7. The deduction allowed to a customer for an early payment of his account is known as a
   A. cash discount
   B. mark down
   C. credit memorandum
   D. trade discount

   7.___

8. In a C.O.D. freight shipment, the business form that the seller attaches to the bill of lading is a
   A. sight draft
   B. promissory note
   C. check
   D. time draft

   8.___

9. The form prepared to test the equality of debits and credits in the General Ledger is called
   A. statement of account
   B. balance sheet
   C. trial balance
   D. income statement

   9.___

10. If the depreciation of a truck is calculated by the 10.____
straight-line method, which statement is CORRECT?
   A. As the truck becomes older, the rate of depreciation
      increases.
   B. The rate of depreciation is the same each year.
   C. The amount of annual depreciation is based on the
      truck's mileage.
   D. On a statement of profit and loss, the depreciation
      appears as a deferred expense.

11. An example of a machine commonly used to record data on 11.____
cards in machine-readable form for use in an automatic
data processing system is the
   A. typewriter   B. electric billing machine
   C. office copying machine   D. key punch

12. An inventory of merchandise prepared from an actual count 12.____
of stock items on hand is described as a(n) _____ inventory.
   A. perpetual   B. physical   C. estimated   D. fixed

13. Which is NOT classified as a current asset on the balance 13.____
sheet?
   A. Petty Cash   B. Notes Receivable
   C. Land   D. Accounts Receivable

14. Which error will cause a trial balance to be out of 14.____
balance?
   A. Failure to post the debit part of a journal entry
   B. Failure to record an entire journal entry
   C. Error in totaling the sales journal
   D. Posting a debit in the debit side of the wrong account

15. If a customer's check which you had deposited is returned 15.____
to you by the bank labeled *dishonored*, what entry would
be made?
Debit
   A. Cash and credit customer's account
   B. Miscellaneous Expense and credit Cash
   C. customer's account and credit Capital
   D. customer's account and credit Cash

16. The total of the Purchases Journal for the month of May 16.____
1980 was incorrectly computed as $6,500. The correct
amount was $5,500. The $6,500 was used to record and
post the summary entry for the month.
To correct the error, the bookkeeper should debit
   A. Merchandise Purchases and credit Accounts Payable
      $5,500
   B. Merchandise Purchases and credit Accounts Payable
      $1,000
   C. Accounts Payable and credit Merchandise Purchases
      $1,000
   D. Accounts Payable and credit Merchandise Purchases
      $6,500

17. Entries in the Purchases Journal are USUALLY recorded from   17.___
    A. purchase requisitions   B. purchase invoices
    C. check stubs   D. credit memorandums

18. Merchandise was sold on April 10, 1988 for $400 less a   18.___
trade discount of 25%, terms 2/10, n/30.
The amount required to settle the invoice on April 20 is
    A. $294   B. $300   C. $392   D. $400

19. When the books were closed at the end of the business   19.___
fiscal year, there was a failure to record depreciation
on Office Equipment for the year.
This error had the effect of
    A. *understating* the book value of the asset Office Equip-
       ment
    B. *overstating* the book value of the asset Office Equip-
       ment
    C. *understating* the net income of the asset Office Equip-
       ment
    D. *overstating* operating expenses

Questions 20-25.

DIRECTIONS: Questions 20 through 25 are to be answered SOLELY on the
basis of the following bank reconciliation statement.

CONDON, INC. Bank Reconciliation March 31, 1970			
Checkbook balance	$3,148.70	Bank Balance	$3,830.65
Less: Service Charge	4.15	Add: Deposit in Transit	310.00
		Total	4,140.65
		Less: Outstanding Checks	
		No. 815 $470.20	
		817 525.90	996.10
		(No. 813 certified 920.00)	
Adjusted checkbook balance	$3,144.55	Available bank balance	$3,144.55

20. Which entry will be made on the books of Condon, Inc. to   20.___
record the bank service charge?
Debit
    A. Cash, credit Bank Charges
    B. Bank Charges, credit Accounts Payable
    C. Bank Charges, credit Cash
    D. Bank Account, credit Bank Charges

21. The deposit in transit of $310 will be listed on the   21.___
    A. bank statement for the month of March
    B. bank statement for the month of April
    C. bank statement for the month of February
    D. check stub record *only*

22. The bookkeeper determined which checks were outstanding   22.____
    by
    A. counting the cancelled checks
    B. examining the bank statement
    C. comparing the cancelled checks with the bank statement
    D. comparing the cancelled checks with the check stubs

23. The certified check of $920 was NOT deducted with the   23.____
    other outstanding checks because it
    A. was deducted from our bank balance at the time it
       was certified
    B. was not deducted from our checkbook balance when it
       was written
    C. will not be cashed by our bank
    D. will not be deducted from our bank balance until it
       clears our bank

24. The MAIN reason for preparing the bank reconciliation   24.____
    statement is to determine the
    A. total amount of cancelled checks
    B. total amount of outstanding checks
    C. total deposits with withdrawals for the month
    D. errors that might have been made

25. A trial balance is prepared to   25.____
    A. see if the totals agree with the subsidiary ledgers
    B. see if the total debit balances in the General Ledger
       agree with the total credit balances in the General
       Ledger
    C. show the worth of the business
    D. make up statements of customers' accounts

_____

KEY (CORRECT ANSWERS)

1. B		11. D	
2. D		12. B	
3. A		13. C	
4. C		14. A	
5. D		15. D	
6. C		16. C	
7. A		17. B	
8. A		18. A	
9. C		19. B	
10. B		20. C	

21. B
22. D
23. A
24. D
25. B

_____

TEST 4

DIRECTIONS: Each question or incomplete statement is followed by several suggested answers or completions. Select the one that BEST answers the question or completes the statement. *PRINT THE LETTER OF THE CORRECT ANSWER IN THE SPACE AT THE RIGHT.*

1. The due date of a 60-day promissory note dated June 15 is August

   A. 13   B. 14   C. 15   D. 16

   1.____

2. Using the information that can be found in the Income Statement, one can find the

   A. current ratio
   B. merchandise turnover
   C. working capital
   D. rate of return on capital

   2.____

3. A machine that is used to record data on cards in a computerized bookkeeping system is the

   A. keypunch machine   B. bookkeeping machine
   C. billing machine   D. sorter

   3.____

4. The ABC Corporation has 100,000 shares of stock outstanding. The Corporation decides to distribute to the stockholders a $200,000 profit.
   If a stockholder owns 100 shares of stock, he will receive a TOTAL dividend of

   A. $50.00   B. $2.00   C. $200.00   D. $.50

   4.____

5. A transaction that will cause a DECREASE in capital is a

   A. purchase of office equipment on credit
   B. payment of a creditor's account less a cash discount
   C. payment of an interest-bearing note
   D. prepayment of freight for a customer, to be charged to the customer's account

   5.____

6. Mr. Davis is married and has three children who go to school. His oldest son, age 17, earned $900 during the year working parttime.
   On his joint Federal income tax return, Mr. Davis may claim a MAXIMUM of _____ exemptions.

   A. five   B. two   C. three   D. four

   6.____

7. If the total of the Schedule of Accounts Receivable does not agree with the balance in the Accounts Receivable Controlling account, the difference may have been caused by

   A. adding the Sales Journal incorrectly
   B. failing to enter a sale in the Sales Journal
   C. posting a sale to the wrong customer's account
   D. failing to record a check received from a customer

   7.____

8. An entry in the general journal is USUALLY made from the   8.___
    A. sales invoice   B. purchase invoice
    C. credit memorandum   D. incoming check

9. An example of a tax collected by the Federal government   9.___
    is the
    A. sales tax
    B. real estate tax
    C. automobile registration fee
    D. social security tax

10. The adjusting entry at the end of the year to record the   10.___
    estimated depreciation for the year results in a(n)
    A. *increase* in liabilities and a decrease in capital
    B. *decrease* in assets and an increase in assets
    C. *decrease* in assets and a decrease in capital
    D. *decrease* in assets and an increase in capital

11. On December 28, the total in the Salaries Expense Account   11.___
    was $59,500. On December 31, the bookkeeper recorded
    accrued salaries of $600.
    The entry to close the Salaries Expense Account on
    December 31 should be debit the _____ and credit the _____.
    A. Income and Expense Summary Account for $59,500;
        Salaries Expense Account for $59,500
    B. Income and Expense Summary Account for $60,100;
        Salaries Expense Account for $60,100
    C. Income and Expense Summary Account for $58,900;
        Salaries Expense Account for $58,900
    D. Salaries Expense Account for $59,500; Income and
        Expense Summary Account for $59,500

12. The tax paid by the employee to provide benefits upon his   12.___
    retirement is the
    A. FICA tax
    B. State Disability Benefits
    C. Federal withholding tax
    D. workmen's compensation insurance

13. The Federal income tax form that is given to the employee   13.___
    to show his total salary for the year and the amount of
    withholding tax for the year is called Form
    A. 941   B. W-4   C. 1099   D. W-2

14. An error that would cause the trial balance to be out of   14.___
    balance would be INCORRECTLY adding
    A. the Purchase Journal
    B. the cash column in the Cash Receipts Journal
    C. the Schedule of Accounts Receivable
    D. extensions on an invoice

15. An account that would be shown in a post-closing trial   15.___
    balance is
    A. Notes Receivable   B. Sales Income
    C. Discount on Purchases   D. Freight Out

16. You have just posted an entry from the Sales Journal to the customer's account. The correct amount in the Sales Journal is $125, but you posted $12.50.
To correct the error, you should
   A. draw a single line through the $12.50 in the account and write $125 above it
   B. debit in the General Journal the customer's account for $112.50 and credit the Sales Income Account for $112.50
   C. credit in the General Journal the customer's account for $12.50 and debit the Sales Income Account for $12.50
   D. debit in the Sales Journal the customer's account for $112.50 and credit the Sales Income Account for $112.50

16.___

17. When the bookkeeper added the trial balance, she found that it did not balance.
To find the reason, a logical FIRST step would be to
   A. check the pencil footings in ledger accounts
   B. add the trial balance a second time
   C. check whether figures were copied correctly from the ledger to the trial balance
   D. check postings from the journals

17.___

18. A column or group of columns containing data of a specific nature on a punched card is called a
   A. zone   B. field   C. row   D. file

18.___

19. *Allowance for Doubtful Accounts* is BEST described as a(n) _____ account.
   A. contingent liability   B. capital
   C. expense   D. asset valuation

19.___

20. A sales invoice to Judy Burns for $50 was entered in the Sales Journal as $150.
Which would occur as a result of this error?
The
   A. trial balance will not balance at the end of the month
   B. balance of the monthly statement to Judy Burns will be overstated
   C. check received from Judy Burns in payment of her account will be larger than the correct amount
   D. Accounts Receivable controlling account will not agree with the Schedule of Accounts Receivable at the end of the month

20.___

21. Sales taxes which are collected from customers and which will subsequently be remitted to the State Tax Bureau are recorded by the retailer as a(n)
   A. operating expense in the Income Statement
   B. addition to sales in the Income Statement
   C. current asset in the Balance Sheet
   D. current liability in the Balance Sheet

21.___

22. When the payee of a check writes as an endorsement *Pay to the order of (name of the firm)* before his signature, he has used a _____ endorsement.
    A. blank   B. qualified
    C. restrictive   D. full

22.___

23. Entries in the Purchases Journal are USUALLY made from which source document?
    A. Purchase order   B. Purchase requisition
    C. Incoming invoice   D. Outgoing invoice

23.___

24. Which is shown on the bank statement sent by the bank each month?
    A. Outstanding checks
    B. Deposits in transit
    C. Checks paid by the bank during the month
    D. The amount of interest earned during the month

24.___

25. The authorization by the State of New York which permits a group of persons to do business as a corporation is called the
    A. charter   B. by-laws
    C. trade acceptance   D. articles of copartnership

25.___

KEY (CORRECT ANSWERS)

1. B		11. B
2. B		12. A
3. A		13. D
4. C		14. B
5. C		15. A
6. A		16. A
7. A		17. B
8. C		18. B
9. D		19. D
10. C		20. B

21. D
22. D
23. C
24. C
25. A

EXAMINATION SECTION
TEST 1

DIRECTIONS: Each question or incomplete statement is followed by several suggested answers or completions. Select the one that BEST answers the question or completes the statement. *PRINT THE LETTER OF THE CORRECT ANSWER IN THE SPACE AT THE RIGHT.*

1. In the preparation of a balance sheet, failure to consider the inventory of office supplies will result in _____ assets and _____.   1.____

    A. overstating; overstating liabilities
    B. understating; overstating capital
    C. understating; understating capital
    D. overstating; understating liabilities

2. The annual federal unemployment tax is paid by the   2.____

    A. employer *only*
    B. employee *only*
    C. employer and the employee equally
    D. employee, up to a maximum of 30 cents per week, and the balance is paid by the employer

3. Which are NORMALLY considered as current assets?   3.____

    A. Bank overdrafts   B. Prepaid expenses
    C. Accrued expenses   D. Payroll taxes

4. What type of ledger account is a summary of a number of accounts in another ledger? The _____ account.   4.____

    A. controlling   B. subsidiary
    C. asset   D. proprietorship

5. The PRIMARY purpose of a petty cash fund is to   5.____

    A. provide a fund for paying all miscellaneous expenses
    B. take the place of the cash account
    C. provide a common drawing fund for the owners of the business
    D. avoid entering a number of small amounts in the Cash Payments Journal

6. In the absence of a written agreement, profits in a partnership would be divided   6.____

    A. in proportion to the investment of the partners
    B. on an equitable basis depending on the time and effort spent by the partners
    C. equally
    D. on a ratio of investment basis, giving the senior partner preference

7. Which account represents a subtraction or decrease to an income account?   7.____

    A. Purchase Returns & Allowances
    B. Sales Returns & Allowances
    C. Freight In
    D. Prepaid Rent

8. If the Interest Expense account showed a debit balance of $210 as of December 31, and $40 of this amount was prepaid on Notes Payable, which statement is CORRECT as of December 31?   8.___

    A. Prepaid Interest of $170 should be shown as a deferred expense in the balance sheet.
    B. Interest Expense should be shown in the Income Statement as $210.
    C. Prepaid Interest of $40 should be listed as a deferred credit to income in the balance sheet.
    D. Interest Expense should be shown in the Income Statement as $170.

9. When prices are rising, which inventory-valuation method results in the LOWEST inventory value?   9.___

    A. FIFO
    C. Average cost
    B. LIFO
    D. Declining balance

10. Which of the following is a CORRECT procedure in preparing a bank reconciliation?   10.___

    A. Deposits in transit should be added to the cash balance on the books, and outstanding checks should be deducted from the cash balance on the bank statement.
    B. The cash balance on the bank statement and the cash balance on the books should be equal if there are deposits in transit and outstanding checks.
    C. Outstanding checks should be deducted from the cash balance on the books.
    D. Any service charge should be deducted from the check stub balance.

11. Which ratio indicates that there may NOT be enough on hand to meet current obligations?   11.___

    A. $\dfrac{\text{fixed assets}}{\text{fixed liabilities}} = \dfrac{2}{3}$
    B. $\dfrac{\text{total assets}}{\text{total obligations}} = \dfrac{3}{5}$

    C. $\dfrac{\text{current assets}}{\text{current liabilities}} = \dfrac{1}{3}$
    D. $\dfrac{\text{current assets}}{\text{fixed liabilities}} = \dfrac{1}{2}$

12. Which asset is NOT subject to depreciation?   12.___

    A. Factory equipment
    C. Buildings
    B. Land
    D. Machinery

13. Which form is prepared to verify that the total of the account balances in the Customers Ledger agrees with the balance in the controlling account in the General Ledger?   13.___

    A. Worksheet
    B. Schedule of accounts payable
    C. Schedule of accounts receivable
    D. Trial balance

14. If the merchandise inventory on hand at the end of the year was overstated, what will be   14._____
the result of this error?

    A. *Understatement* of income for the year
    B. *Overstatement* of income for the year
    C. *Understatement* of assets at the end of the year
    D. No effect on income or assets

15. Working capital is found by subtracting the total current liabilities from the total   15._____

    A. fixed liabilities   B. fixed assets
    C. current income   D. current assets

16. Which is the CORRECT procedure for calculating the rate of merchandise turnover?   16._____

    A. Gross Sales divided by Net Sales
    B. Cost of Sales divided by Average Inventory
    C. Net Purchases divided by Average Inventory
    D. Gross Purchases divided by Net Purchases

17. The books of the Atlas Cement Corporation show a net profit of $142,000.   17._____
To close the Profit and Loss account of the corporation at the end of the year, the
account CREDITED should be

    A. Earned Surplus   B. Capital Stock
    C. C. Atlas, Capital   D. C. Atlas, Personal

18. The bank statement at the end of the month indicated a bank charge for printing a new   18._____
checkbook.
How is this information recorded?
Debit

    A. Cash and credit Office Supplies
    B. Office Supplies and credit the Bank Charges
    C. the Bank Charges and credit Office Supplies
    D. Miscellaneous Expense and credit Cash

19. The Allowance for Doubtful Accounts appears on the balance sheet as a deduction from   19._____

    A. Accounts Receivable   B. Notes Receivable
    C. Accounts Payable   D. Notes Payable

20. The Tucker Equipment Corporation had a $45,000 profit for the year ended December   20._____
31.
Which would be the PROPER entry to close the Income and Expense account at the end
of the year?
Debit Income and Expense Summary; credit

    A. Tucker, Capital   B. Tucker, Drawing
    C. Retained Earnings   D. Capital Stock

21. A failure to record a purchases invoice would be discovered when the 21.

    A. monthly statement of account is sent to the customer
    B. check is received from the customer
    C. check is sent to the creditor
    D. statement of account is received from the creditor

22. Which General Ledger account would appear in a post-closing trial balance? 22.

    A. Notes Receivable   B. Bad Debts Expense
    C. Sales Discount   D. Fee Income

23. Which deduction is affected by the number of exemptions claimed? 23.

    A. State Disability   B. State income tax
    C. FICA tax   D. Workers' Compensation

24. The face value of a 60-day, 12% promissory note is $900. 24.
The maturity value of this note will be

    A. $909   B. $900   C. $918   D. $1,008

25. An invoice dated March 10, terms 2/10, n/30, should be paid no later than 25.

    A. March 20   B. March 31   C. April 9   D. April 10

KEY (CORRECT ANSWERS)

1. C		11. C	
2. A		12. B	
3. B		13. C	
4. A		14. B	
5. D		15. D	
6. C		16. B	
7. B		17. A	
8. D		18. D	
9. B		19. A	
10. D		20. C	

21. D
22. A
23. B
24. C
25. C

TEST 2

DIRECTIONS: Each question or incomplete statement is followed by several suggested answers or completions. Select the one that BEST answers the question or completes the statement. *PRINT THE LETTER OF THE CORRECT ANSWER IN THE SPACE AT THE RIGHT.*

1. Which is NOT an essential element of a computer system?   1.____

   A. Input   B. Central processing unit
   C. Verifier   D. Output

2. The general ledger account that would NOT appear in a post-closing trial balance would   2.____
   be

   A. Cash   B. Accounts Payable
   C. Furniture and Fixtures   D. Sales Income

3. Ralph Hanley, age 45, supports his wife and three children.   3.____
   Mr. Hanley is the only member of the family required to file an income tax return.
   What is the MAXIMUM number of exemptions he can claim?

   A. One   B. Five   C. Three   D. Four

4. The cost of a fixed asset minus the allowance for depreciation (accumulated deprecia-   4.____
   tion) is the _____ value.

   A. market   B. cost   C. liquidation   D. book

5. The form used by a bookkeeper in summarizing adjustments and information which will   5.____
   be used in preparing statements is called a

   A. journal   B. balance sheet
   C. ledger   D. worksheet

6. When a large number of transactions of a particular kind are to be entered in bookkeep-   6.____
   ing records, it is USUALLY advisable to use

   A. cash records   B. controlling accounts
   C. special journals   D. special ledgers

7. The petty cash book shows a petty cash balance of $9.80 on May 31. The petty cash box   7.____
   contains only $9.10.
   What account will be debited to record the $.70 difference?

   A. Cash   B. Petty Cash
   C. Cash Short and Over   D. Petty Cash Expense

8. The ONLY difference between the books of a partnership and those of a sole proprietor-   8.____
   ship appears in the _____ accounts.

   A. proprietorship   B. liability
   C. asset   D. expense

9. The earnings of a corporation are FIRST recorded as a credit to an account called   9.____

   A. Dividends Payable   B. Capital Stock Authorized
   C. Retained Earnings   D. Profit and Loss Summary

10. A firm purchased a new delivery truck for $2,900 and sold it four years later for $500. The   10.
Allowance for Depreciation of Delivery Equipment account was credited for $580 at the
end of each of the four years.
When the machine was sold, there was a

A. loss of $80   B. loss of $1,820
C. loss of $2,400   D. gain of $80

11. FICA taxes are paid by   11.

A. employees *only*
B. employers *only*
C. both employees and employers
D. neither employees nor employers

12. Which phase of the data processing cycle is the SAME as calculating net pay in a man-   12.
ual system?

A. Input   B. Processing   C. Storing   D. Output

13. Which error will cause the trial balance to be out of balance?   13.

A. A sales invoice for $60 was entered in the Sales Journal for $600.
B. A credit to office furniture in the journal was posted as a credit to office machines in
the ledger.
C. A debit to advertising expense in the journal was posted as a debit to miscellaneous expense in the ledger.
D. A debit to office equipment in the journal was posted as a credit to office equipment
in the ledger.

14. The collection of a bad debt previously written off will result in a(n)   14.

A. *decrease* in assets   B. *decrease* in capital
C. *increase* in assets   D. *increase* in liabilities

15. Which account does NOT belong in the group?   15.

A. Notes Receivable   B. Building
C. Office Equipment   D. Delivery Truck

16. The adjusting entry to record the estimated bad debts is debit _____ and credit   16.
_____.

A. Allowance for Bad Debts; Bad Debts Expense
B. Bad Debts Expense; Allowance for Bad Debts
C. Allowance for Bad Debts; Accounts Receivable
D. Bad Debts Expense; Accounts Receivable

17. At the end of the year, which account should be closed into the income and expense   17.
summary?

A. Freight In   B. Allowance for Doubtful Accounts
C. Notes Receivable   D. Petty Cash

18. Which form is prepared to aid in verifying that the customer's account balances in the customer's ledger agree with the balance in the Accounts Receivable account in the general ledger?

    A. Worksheet
    B. Schedule of Accounts Payable
    C. Schedule of Accounts Receivable
    D. Trial Balance

18._____

19. In the preparation of an income statement, failure to consider accrued wages will result in

    A. *overstating* operating expense and understating net profit
    B. *overstating* net profit *only*
    C. *understating* operating expense and overstating net profit
    D. *understating* operating expense *only*

19._____

20. The CORRECT formula for determining the rate of merchandise turnover is

    A. cost of goods sold divided by average inventory
    B. net sales divided by net purchases
    C. gross sales divided by ending inventory
    D. average inventory divided by cost of goods sold

20._____

21. A legal characteristic of a corporation is _____ liability.

    A. contingent   B. limited
    C. unlimited   D. deferred

21._____

22. A customer's check you had deposited is returned to you by the bank labeled *Dishonored.*
What entries would be made as a result of this action? Debit _____ and credit _____.

    A. cash; customer's account
    B. miscellaneous expense; cash
    C. customer's account; capital
    D. customer's account; cash

22._____

23. The TOTAL capital of a corporation may be found by adding

    A. assets and liabilities
    B. assets and capital stock
    C. liabilities and capital stock
    D. earned surplus and capital stock

23._____

24. The source of an entry made in the Petty Cash book is the

    A. general ledger   B. voucher
    C. register   D. general journal

24._____

25. Which account is debited to record interest earned but not yet due?

    A. Deferred Interest
    B. Interest Receivable
    C. Interest Income
    D. Income and Expense Summary

25._____

KEY (CORRECT ANSWERS)

1.	C	11.	C
2.	D	12.	B
3.	B	13.	D
4.	D	14.	C
5.	D	15.	A
6.	C	16.	B
7.	C	17.	A
8.	A	18.	C
9.	C	19.	C
10.	A	20.	A

21.	B
22.	D
23.	D
24.	B
25.	B

———

TEST 3

DIRECTIONS: Each question or incomplete statement is followed by several suggested answers or completions. Select the one that BEST answers the question or completes the statement. *PRINT THE LETTER OF THE CORRECT ANSWER IN THE SPACE AT THE RIGHT.*

1. Which reason should NOT generally be used by an employer when making a hiring deci-   1.____
   sion?
   An applicant('s)

   A. resume reveals a lack of job-related skills
   B. attendance record on a previous job is poor
   C. has improperly prepared the job application
   D. is married

2. Graves, Owens, and Smith formed a partnership and invested $15,000 each.   2.____
   If the firm made a profit of $18,000 last year and profits and losses were shared equally,
   what was Owens' share of the net profit?

   A. $1,000   B. $5,000   C. $6,000   D. $9,000

3. The bank statement balance of the Bedford Co. on May 31 was $3,263.28. The check-   3.____
   book balance was $3,119.06. A reconciliation showed that the outstanding checks
   totaled $147.22 and that there was a bank service charge of $3.00. The CORRECT
   checkbook balance should be

   A. $3,260.28   B. $3,122.06   C. $3,116.06   D. $3,266.28

4. Which account is shown in a post-closing trial balance?   4.____

   A. Prepaid Insurance   B. Fees Income
   C. Purchases   D. Freight In

5. A check endorsed *For deposit only (signed) Samuel Jones* is an example of a _____   5.____
   endorsement.

   A. full   B. blank   C. complete   D. restrictive

6. The selling price of a share of stock as published in a daily newspaper is called the   6.____
   _____ value.

   A. book   B. face   C. par   D. market

7. Which is obtained by dividing the cost of goods sold by the average inventory?   7.____

   A. Current ratio
   B. Merchandise inventory turnover
   C. Average rate of mark-up
   D. Acid-test ratio

8. A Suzuki truck costing $39,000 is expected to have a useful life of six years and a   8.____
   salvage value of $3,000.
   If $6,000 is debited to the depreciation expense account each year for six years, what
   method of depreciation is used?

   A. Units of production   B. Straight line
   C. Declining balance   D. Sum of the years digits

9. Which form is prepared to aid in verifying that the customer's account balances in the customer's ledger agree with the balance in the Accounts Receivable account in the General Ledger?

    A. Worksheet
    B. Schedule of Accounts Payable
    C. Schedule of Accounts Receivable
    D. Trial Balance

10. In the preparation of a balance sheet, failure to consider commissions owed to salespersons will result in _____ liabilities and _____ capital.

    A. understating; overstating
    B. understating; understating
    C. overstating; overstating
    D. overstating; understating

11. A financial statement generated by a computer is an example of a(n)

    A. audit trail   B. output
    C. input   D. program

12. Merchandise was sold for $150 cash plus a 3% sales tax.
The CORRECT credit(s) should be

    A. Sales Income $150, Sales Taxes Payable $4.50
    B. Sales Income $154.50
    C. Merchandise $150, Sales Taxes Payable $4.50
    D. Sales Income $150

13. The bookkeeper should prepare a bank reconciliation MAINLY to determine

    A. which checks are outstanding
    B. whether the checkbook balance and the bank statement balance are in agreement
    C. the total amount of checks written during the month
    D. the total amount of cash deposited during the month

14. Which is the CORRECT procedure for calculating the rate of merchandise turnover?

    A. Gross Sales divided by Net Sales
    B. Cost of Goods Sold divided by Average Inventory
    C. Net Purchases divided by Average Inventory
    D. Gross Purchases divided by Net Purchases

15. Which previous job should be listed FIRST on a job application form?
The

    A. least recent job   B. most recent job
    C. job you liked best   D. job which paid the most

16. Failure to record cash sales will result in

    A. *overstatement* of profit
    B. *understatement* of profit
    C. *understatement* of liabilities
    D. *overstatement* of capital

17. When a fixed asset is repaired, the cost of the repairs should be _____ account.　　17.____

    A. *debited* to the asset
    B. *debited* to the expense
    C. *credited* to the proprietor's capital
    D. *credited* to the asset

18. The form used by a bookkeeper to summarize information which will be used in prepar-　　18.____
ing financial statements is called a

    A. journal　　　　　　　　　　　　B. balance sheet
    C. ledger　　　　　　　　　　　　D. worksheet

19. Which type of ledger account is a summary of a number of accounts in another ledger?　　19.____
_____ account.

    A. Controlling　　　　　　　　　　B. Subsidiary
    C. Asset　　　　　　　　　　　　　D. Proprietorship

20. What is the summary entry on the Purchases Journal?　　20.____
Debit _____ and credit _____.

    A. Accounts Payable; Merchandise Purchases
    B. Accounts Receivable; Merchandise Purchases
    C. Merchandise Purchases; Accounts Receivable
    D. Merchandise Purchases; Accounts Payable

21. The source document for entries made in the Sales Journal is a(n)　　21.____

    A. credit memo　　　　　　　　　　B. statement of accounts
    C. invoice　　　　　　　　　　　　D. bill of lading

22. A Trial Balance which is in balance would NOT reveal the　　22.____

    A. omission of the credit part of an entry
    B. posting of the same debit twice
    C. omission of an entire transaction
    D. omission of an account with a balance

23. A financial statement prepared by a computerized accounting system is an example of　　23.____

    A. input　　　　　　　　　　　　　B. output
    C. flowcharting　　　　　　　　　　D. programming

24. The form which the payroll clerk gives to each employee to show gross earnings and　　24.____
taxes withheld for the year is a

    A. W-2　　　　B. W-3　　　　C. W-4　　　　D. 1040

25. Who would be the LEAST appropriate reference on an application for a job?　　25.____
A

    A. relative
    B. guidance counselor
    C. former employer
    D. prominent member of the community

KEY (CORRECT ANSWERS)

1.	D	11.	B
2.	C	12.	A
3.	C	13.	B
4.	A	14.	B
5.	D	15.	B
6.	D	16.	B
7.	B	17.	B
8.	B	18.	D
9.	C	19.	A
10.	A	20.	D

21.	C
22.	C
23.	B
24.	A
25.	A

EXAMINATION SECTION
TEST 1

DIRECTIONS: Each question or incomplete statement is followed by several suggested answers or completions. Select the one that BEST answers the question or completes the statement. *PRINT THE LETTER OF THE CORRECT ANSWER IN THE SPACE AT THE RIGHT.*

Questions 1-7.

DIRECTIONS: Questions 1 through 7 are to be answered on the basis of the following income statement.

Laura Lee's Bridal Shop
Income Statement
For the Year Ended December 31, 2005

Revenue:
New & Used Bridal Gowns & Accessories $55,000

Expenses:
Advertisement Expense $ 2,000
Salaries Expense   12,000
Dry cleaning & Alterations   10,000
Utilities   1,500
Total Expenses   25,500

Net Income $29,500

1. What is the period of time covered by this income statement?   1.___
   A. January-December 2004
   B. December 2005
   C. January 2004-December 2005
   D. January-December 2005

2. What is the source of the revenue?   2.___
   A. New and used bridal gowns, advertisements, salaries, dry cleaning, and utilities
   B. Advertisements, salaries, dry cleaning, alterations, and utilities
   C. New and used bridal gowns and accessories
   D. Net income

3. What is the total revenue?   3.___
   A. $25,500   B. $55,000   C. $29,500   D. $79,500

4. Which of the following are expenses?   4.___
   A. Salaries
   B. New and used bridal gowns and accessories
   C. Revenue
   D. New and used bridal gowns, advertisements, and dry cleaning

5. What are the total expenses? 5.___
   A. $55,000   B. $29,500   C. $79,500   D. $25,500

6. There is a resulting net income because 6.___
   A. total revenue and total expenses are combined
   B. net income is greater than total revenue
   C. the total revenue is greater than total expenses
   D. the total revenue is less than total expenses

7. Is this statement an interim statement? 7.___
   A. *Yes*, because it covers an entire accounting period
   B. *No*, because it covers an entire accounting period
   C. *Yes*, because it covers a period of less than a year
   D. *No*, because it covers a period of more than a year

8. What is the name of the accounting report that may show 8.___
   either a net profit or a net loss for an accounting
   period?
   A. Income statement   B. Balance sheet
   C. Statement of capital   D. Classified balance sheet

9. What are the two main parts of the body of the income 9.___
   statement?
   A. Cash and Capital   B. Revenue and Expenses
   C. Liabilities and Capital   D. Assets and Notes Payable

10. If total revenue exceeds total expenses for an accounting 10.___
    period, what is the difference called?
    A. Gross income   B. Total liabilities
    C. Total assets   D. Net income

11. In the body of a balance sheet, what are the three 11.___
    sections called?
    A. Assets and liabilities
    B. Cash, liabilities, and revenue
    C. Assets, liabilities, and capital
    D. Revenue, assets, and capital

12. What business record shows the results of the proprietor's 12.___
    borrowing assets from the business, usually in anticipa-
    tion of profits?
    A. Proprietor's withdrawals
    B. Accounts payable
    C. Liabilities and Capital
    D. Total liabilities

Questions 13-24.

DIRECTIONS: For each transaction given for Mona's Magic Moments
              Hair Salon in Questions 13 through 24, identify
              which journal the transaction should be recorded in.

13. April 1: Mona, the owner, paid the month's rent - $600.00; 13.____
    check no. 356.
    A. General   B. Cash disbursements
    C. Purchases   D. Sales

14. April 6: the salon purchased $300.00 worth of styling   14.____
    products on account from Pomme de Terre Company.
    A. Cash disbursements   B. General
    C. Sales   D. Purchases

15. April 8: sold $100.00 worth of hair products on account 15.____
    to Mrs. Angela Bray.
    A. Sales   B. Purchases
    C. Cash disbursements   D. General

16. April 11: the owner, Mona Ramen, withdrew $80.00 of   16.____
    styling products for personal use.
    A. Sales   B. Cash receipts
    C. General   D. Cash disbursements

17. April 13: paid Pomme de Terre Company $300.00 on   17.____
    account; check 357.
    A. Purchases   B. Cash disbursements
    C. Cash receipts   D. General

18. April 15: cash sales to date were $4,607.00.   18.____
    A. Cash disbursements   B. Purchases
    C. Sales   D. General

19. April 17: issued credit slip #17 to Mrs. Angela Bray   19.____
    for $25.00 for merchandise returned.
    A. Cash disbursements   B. Cash receipts
    C. Sales   D. General

20. April 19: paid electric bill for $250.00; check no. 358. 20.____
    A. Cash disbursements   B. Purchases
    C. General   D. Cash receipts

21. April 21: received $75.00 from Mrs. Angela Bray for   21.____
    balance due on account.
    A. Sales   B. Cash disbursements
    C. Cash receipts   D. Purchases

22. April 23: sold $88.00 of hair products on account to   22.____
    Ms. Tania Alioto.
    A. Purchases   B. Sales
    C. Cash disbursements   D. Cash receipts

23. April 27: purchased $500.00 of equipment from Salon   23.____
    Stylings Merchandisers on account.
    A. Cash disbursements   B. Sales
    C. General   D. Purchases

24. April 30:   cash sales to date were $5023.00.   24.___
        A. Purchases   B. Sales
        C. Cash receipts   D. General

Questions 25-30.

DIRECTIONS: Questions 25 through 30 are to be answered on the
             basis of the following ledger for a barbecue take-out
             restaurant owned and operated by Ruby Joiner.

Cash		Accounts Receivable		Delivery Equipment	
450	150	360	170	5,000	
212	125	250	100	4,000	
328	440	165	120	3,000	
172	125	100	60		
250	70				
275	150				
325	50				

Supplies		Ruby Joiner, Capital		Accounts Payable	
40			8,200	10	600
65			2,000	15	300
30			2,097		200
25					

Ruby Joiner, Drawing		Advertising Expense		Delivery Income	
225		40			400
175		45			350
200					250
					100

Trucking Expense		Telephone Expense	
100		80	
50		40	
		20	

25. What is the balance on the Cash account shown above?   25.___
        A. 2,012.00   B. 1,110.00   C. 3,122.00   D. 902.00

26. What is the balance on the Accounts receivable account   26.___
     shown above?
        A. 425.00   B. 875.00   C. 450.00   D. 1315.00

27. What is the balance on the Accounts payable account   27.___
     shown above?
        A. 1100.00   B. 1075.00   C. 25.00   D. 1125.00

28. Which of the above accounts has a balance of 1100.00?   28.___
        A. Accounts payable   B. Delivery income
        C. Cash   D. Delivery equipment

29. Which of the above accounts has a balance of 12,000.00?   29.____
    A. Ruby Joiner, Capital
    B. Cash and Accounts receivable combined
    C. Delivery equipment
    D. None of the accounts

30. If you made a balance sheet out of the information listed   30.____
    above, Ruby Joiner's total assets would be
    A. 14,472.00   B. 12,297.00   C. 13,392.00   D. 13,487.00

Questions 31-34.

DIRECTIONS: Questions 31 through 34 are to be answered on the
              basis of the following information, to be included
              on a checking deposit ticket.

Five $20 bills; 11 $10 bills; 6 $5 bills; 47 $1 bills; 200 half
dollars; 120 quarters; 112 dimes; 320 nickels; 67 pennies.
Second National Bank (73-124) check of 152.34; Bank of the Midwest
(13-298) check of 68.37; Great National Bank (32-165) check of
185.06.

31. What is the TOTAL currency for this deposit?   31.____
    A. $387   B. $287   C. $444.87   D. $157.87

32. What is the TOTAL coin for this deposit?   32.____
    A. $387   B. $287   C. $444.87   D. $157.87

33. What is the check total for this deposit?   33.____
    A. $692.77   B. $406   C. $405.77   D. $850.64

34. What is the TOTAL deposit?   34.____
    A. $444.87   B. $692.77   C. $851   D. $850.64

Questions 35-37.

DIRECTIONS: Questions 35 through 37 are to be answered on the
              basis of the following petty cash journal.

Date	Receipt No.	To Whom Paid	For What	Acct.#	Amount
10/2	1	Anna Jones - Mail	Postage	548	13.50
10/2	2	Jim Collins	Telegram	525	5.75
10/4	3	Anna Jones - Mail	Postage	548	13.50
10/5	4	Lucky Stores	Coffee	515	7.34
10/6	5	Tom Allen	Lunch w/customer	525	11.38

35. What is the TOTAL disbursement from this fund for the   35.____
    time period 10/1 through 10/6?
    A. $51.47   B. $40.09   C. $61.47   D. $26.59

36. How much money was disbursed to Account #548 during the   36.____
    time period 10/1-10/16?
       A. $51.47   B. $26   C. $27   D. $34.34

37. If the fund began the month with a total of $100.00, what   37.____
    amount was left in the fund at the end of business on
    10/5?
       A. $48.53   B. $59.91   C. $51.47   D. $40.09

Questions 38-40.

DIRECTIONS: Questions 38 through 40 are to be answered on the
              basis of the following information.

    A promissory note dated December 1, 2005, bearing interest at
a rate of 12% and due in 90 days, is sent to a creditor. The face
value of the note is $900.

38. What is the due date of the promissory note?   38.____
       A. January 15, 2006   B. March 1, 2006
       C. February 1, 2006   D. December 31, 2005

39. What is the TOTAL interest that will be earned on the note? 39.____
       A. $27   B. $270   C. $108   D. $10.80

40. What interest will be earned on the note for the old   40.____
    accounting period (December 1-31)?
       A. $90   B. $36   C. $9   D. $3.60

KEY (CORRECT ANSWERS)

1. D	11. C	21. C	31. B
2. C	12. A	22. B	32. D
3. B	13. B	23. D	33. C
4. A	14. D	24. B	34. D
5. D	15. A	25. D	35. A
6. C	16. C	26. A	36. C
7. B	17. B	27. B	37. B
8. A	18. C	28. B	38. B
9. B	19. D	29. C	39. A
10. D	20. A	30. D	40. C

TEST 2

DIRECTIONS: Each question or incomplete statement is followed by several suggested answers or completions. Select the one that BEST answers the question or completes the statement. *PRINT THE LETTER OF THE CORRECT ANSWER IN THE SPACE AT THE RIGHT.*

Questions 1-4.

DIRECTIONS: Questions 1 through 4 are to be answered on the basis of the following information, to be included in a deposit slip.

14 twenty dollar bills	63 quarters
52 ten dollar bills	22 dimes
12 five dollar bills	44 nickels
43 one dollar bills	70 pennies

Checks: $236.34 and $129.72

1. What is the TOTAL amount of currency for this deposit?   1.____
   A. $923.85   B. $1269.06   C. $903.00   D. $1299.91

2. What is the TOTAL amount of coin for this deposit?   2.____
   A. $20.85   B. $923.85   C. $903.00   D. $1299.91

3. What is the TOTAL amount of check for this deposit?   3.____
   A. $20.85   B. $366.06   C. $1299.91   D. $903.00

4. What is the TOTAL deposit for this slip?   4.____
   A. $1269.06   B. $903.00   C. $923.85   D. $1289.91

Questions 5-7.

DIRECTIONS: Questions 5 through 7 are to be answered on the basis of the following information.

Angela Martinez' last check stub balance was $675.50. Her bank statement balance dated April 30 was $652.00. A $250 deposit was in transit on that date. Outstanding checks were as follows: No. 127, $65.00; No. 129, $203.50; No. 130, $50.00. The bank service charge for the month was $5.00.

5. What was Angela Martinez' available checkbook balance on   5.____
   April 30?
   A. $652.00   B. $338.50   C. $583.50   D. $675.50

6. In order to reconcile her checkbook balance with her bank   6.___
   statement balance, what must Angela Martinez do?
   A. Add her checkbook balance to the balance on her bank
      statement
   B. Subtract her checkbook balance from the balance on
      her bank statement
   C. Ignore her checkbook balance and adopt the balance
      on her bank statement
   D. Adjust the checkbook balance by adding deposits and
      debiting outstanding checks and charges

7. The check stub balance referred to in the problem refers   7.___
   to the
   A. last check Angela Martinez recorded in her checkbook
   B. amount of money left in Angela Martinez' account
      according to her own calculations based on the checks,
      charges, and deposits she has written and recorded,
   C. amount of money left in Angela Martinez' account
      according to the bank's calculations based on the
      checks, charges, and deposits posted to her account,
   D. number of checks left in her checkbook

Questions 8-9.

DIRECTIONS: Questions 8 and 9 are to be answered on the basis of
              the following information.

    Tu Nguyen, an interior designer, received his June bank state-
ment on July 2. The balance was $622.66. His last check stub
balance was $700. On comparing the two, he noticed that a deposit
of $275 made on January 30 was not included on the statement;
also, a bank service charge of $4 was deducted. Outstanding checks
were as follows: No. 331, $97.50; No. 332, $207; No. 335, $25.40;
and No. 336, $68.97.

8. What is Nguyen's CORRECT available bank balance?   8.___
   A. $494.79   B. $897.66   C. $700.00   D. $219.79

9. The bank statement balance referred to in the problem   9.___
   refers to the
   A. last check Tu Nguyen recorded in his checkbook,
   B. last check presented for payment to Tu Nguyen's
      account,
   C. amount of money left in Tu Nguyen's account according
      to the bank's calculations based on the checks,
      charges, and deposits posted to his account,
   D. amount of money left in Tu Nguyen's account based
      on his own calculations of the checks, charges, and
      deposits he has written and recorded

10. What of the following endorsements would be an example of   10.___
    a simple Endorsement in Blank?
       A. Pay to the Order of Joanie Anderson
       B. Joanie Anderson
       C. For deposit only; Acct. No. 12345; Joanie Anderson
       D. Without Recourse; Joanie Anderson

11. Which of the following endorsements would limit the   11.___
    further purpose or use of the endorsed check?
       A. Pay to the Order of Joanie Anderson
       B. Joanie Anderson
       C. For deposit only; Acct. No. 12345; Joanie Anderson
       D. Without Recourse; Joanie Anderson

12. Which of the following endorsements would protect the   12.___
    endorser from legal responsibility for payment, should
    the drawer have insufficient funds to honor his/her own
    check?
       A. Pay to the Order of Joanie Anderson
       B. Joanie Anderson
       C. For deposit only; Acct. No. 12345; Joanie Anderson
       D. Without Recourse; Joanie Anderson

Questions 13-24.

DIRECTIONS: Questions 13 - 24 are to be answered on the basis
              of the following ledger accounts for Wheelsmith
              Organic Farms.

Wheelsmith Organic Farms
Ledger Accounts

Cash	Accounts Payable	Service Supplies
2006	2006	2006
Jan. 1	Jan. 1	Jan. 1
4,000	2,000	2,000

Shelley Wheelsmith, Capital	Machinery
2006	2006
Jan. 1	Jan. 1
11,000	7,000

13. Transaction #1: On January 5, Shelley Wheelsmith, the   13.___
    proprietor, received cash amounting to $5,000 as a result
    of returning machinery that had recently been purchased.
    What account(s) should this transaction be posted to?
       A. Cash
       B. Cash and Machinery
       C. Machinery
       D. Cash, Machinery, and Service Supplies

14. Transaction #2: On January 8, Shelley Wheelsmith, the   14.____
proprietor, sent out a check for $600 in partial payment
of the accounts payable.
What account(s) should this transaction be posted to?
A. Accounts Payable
B. Accounts Payable and Cash
C. Accounts Payable and Capital
D. Cash

15. Transaction #3: On January 14, Shelley Wheelsmith,   15.____
proprietor, made an additional investment in the business
by contributing machinery valued at $1,500.
What account(s) should this transaction be posted to?
A. Machinery   B. Machinery and Capital
C. Capital   D. Machinery and Cash

16. Transaction #4: On January 26, Shelley Wheelsmith,   16.____
proprietor, purchased additional service supplies for
$200. She agreed to pay the obligation in 30 days.
What account(s) should this transaction be posted to?
A. Accounts Payable and Liabilities
B. Service supplies
C. Accounts Payable
D. Accounts Payable and Service supplies

17. Transaction #5: On January 31, Shelley Wheelsmith,   17.____
proprietor, purchased service supplies paying cash of $50.
What account(s) should this transaction be posted to?
A. Service supplies
B. Service supplies and Accounts Payable
C. Cash and Service supplies
D. Cash

18. What is the balance in the Cash account after all of these   18.____
transactions are posted?
A. $9,000   B. $1,000   C. $5,000   D. $8,350

19. What is the balance in the Machinery account after all of   19.____
these transactions are posted?
A. $7,000   B. $5,000   C. $3,500   D. $13,500

20. What is the balance in the Accounts Payable account after   20.____
all of these transactions are posted?
A. $800   B. $600   C. $2,600   D. $1,600

21. What is the balance in the Capital account after all of   21.____
these transactions are posted?
A. $12,500   B. $800   C. $11,600   D. $10,400

22. What is the balance in the Service supplies account after   22.____
all of these transactions are posted?
A. $2,000   B. $2,250   C. $750   D. $2,200

23. What are the total assets of Wheelsmith Organic Farms   23.___
    after these transactions have been posted?
       A. $10,600   B. $11,850   C. $14,100   D. $10,750

24. What are the total liabilities and capital for Wheelsmith   24.___
    Organic Farms after these transactions have been posted?
       A. $14,100   B. $12,500   C. $11,850   D. $10,600

Questions 25-28.

DIRECTIONS: Questions 25 through 28 are to be answered on the
            basis of the following information.

     At the end of an accounting period, Andy's Framing Gallery
recorded the following information: Sales, $125,225; Merchandise
Inventory, December 31, 2005, $95,325; Purchases Returns and
Allowances, $3,500; Merchandise Inventory, January 1, 2005,
$98,725; Freight on Purchases, $2,500; Purchases, $120,000.

25. What are the net purchases for Andy's Framing Gallery   25.___
    during the accounting period?
       A. $120,000   B. $119,000   C. $3,500   D. $122,500

26. What is the cost of goods available for sale?   26.___
       A. $119,000   B. $98,725   C. $95,325   D. $217,725

27. What is the total cost of goods sold for this accounting   27.___
    period?
       A. $217,725   B. $95,325   C. $122,400   D. $125,225

28. What is the gross profit on sales for this accounting   28.___
    period?
       A. $2825   B. $2500   C. $125,225   D. $122,400

Questions 29-40.

DIRECTIONS: Questions 29 through 40 are to be answered on the
            basis of the following information.

     The Joie de Vivre Co. received the promissory notes listed
below during the last quarter of its calendar year:

	Date	Face Amount	Terms	Interest Rate	Date Discounted	Discount Rate
(1)	10/8	$3,600	30 days	-	10/18	9%
(2)	9/22	$8,000	60 days	6%	10/1	7%
(3)	11/15	$3,000	90 days	7%	11/20	8%

29. What is the due date for the first note?   29.___
       A. 12/31   B. 11/7   C. 12/7   D. 10/31

30. What interest will be due when the first note matures?   30.____
    A. $3   B. $3,600   C. $30   D. $0

31. What is the maturity value of the first note?   31.____
    A. $3,600   B. $3,630   C. $0   D. $3,603

32. What is the discount period for the first note?   32.____
    A. One fiscal year   B. 10 days
    C. 20 days   D. One month

33. What is the due date for the second note?   33.____
    A. 12/21   B. 11/21   C. 10/21   D. 1/21

34. What interest will be due when the second note matures?   34.____
    A. $60   B. $800.00   C. $8.00   D. $80.00

35. What is the maturity value of the second note?   35.____
    A. $8,000   B. $8,080   C. $8,800   D. $8,008

36. What is the discount period for the second note?   36.____
    A. 51 days   B. 10 days   C. 360 days   D. 60 days

37. What is the due date for the third note?   37.____
    A. 1/14   B. 12/15   C. 12/31   D. 2/13

38. What interest will be due when the third note matures?   38.____
    A. $5.25   B. $52.50   C. $525   D. $90

39. What is the maturity value of the third note?   39.____
    A. $3525   B. $3005.25   C. $3052.50   D. $3090

40. What is the discount period for the third note?   40.____
    A. 60 days   B. 85 days   C. 5 days   D. 90 days

————

KEY (CORRECT ANSWERS)

1. C	11. C	21. A	31. A
2. A	12. D	22. B	32. C
3. B	13. B	23. C	33. B
4. D	14. B	24. A	34. D
5. C	15. B	25. B	35. B
6. D	16. D	26. D	36. A
7. B	17. C	27. C	37. D
8. A	18. D	28. A	38. B
9. C	19. C	29. B	39. C
10. B	20. D	30. D	40. B

TEST 3

DIRECTIONS: Each question or incomplete statement is followed by
              several suggested answers or completions. Select the
              one that BEST answers the question or completes the
              statement. *PRINT THE LETTER OF THE CORRECT ANSWER IN
              THE SPACE AT THE RIGHT.*

Questions 1-8.

DIRECTIONS: Questions 1 through 8 are to be answered on the basis
              of the following Balance Sheet.

Laura Lee's Bridal Shop
Balance Sheet
December 31, 2005

Assets

Cash	$14,000	
Accounts Receivable	3,000	
Bridal Accessories	10,000	
Gowns and Other Inventory	30,000	
Total Assets		$57,000

Liabilities and Capital

Accounts Payable	$ 4,000	
Notes Payable	28,000	
Total Liabilities		$32,000
Laura Lee, Capital		25,000
Total Liabilities and Capital		$57,000

1. When was the balance sheet prepared?   1.____
    A. January 2006
    B. December 31, 2005
    C. After the close of the 2005 fiscal year
    D. December 1, 2005

2. How does the date on this balance sheet differ from the   2.____
    date on the statement of capital or income statement?
    A. It doesn't differ. The dates for each statement
       signify the same time period.
    B. The date on a balance sheet represents the period
       during which any changes indicated on the statement
       took place, whereas the other financial statements
       represent the moment in time when the statement was
       prepared.
    C. The date on a balance sheet represents the moment in
       time when the statement was prepared, whereas the
       other financial statements represent the period during
       which any changes indicated on the statement took
       place.

D. The date on a balance sheet indicates an entire year, whereas the dates on the other statements indicate a single month.

3. Can Laura Lee purchase more bridal gowns for the business paying cash of $16,000?   3.____
   A. *No*, because the business has only $14,000 cash available
   B. *Yes*, because the business has $57,000 cash available
   C. *Yes*, because the business has $57,000 available in assets
   D. *No*, because the business has $57,000 in liabilities

4. What is the owner's equity of Laura Lee's Bridal Shop? Since total equity consists of total _____ total equity is _____.   4.____
   A. assets minus total liabilities and proprietor's capital,; $0
   B. assets minus total liabilities,; $25,000
   C. assets,; $57,000
   D. liabilities and proprietor's capital,; $57,000

5. What is the TOTAL amount of Laura Lee's claim against the total assets of the business?   5.____
   A. $57,000   B. $25,000   C. $0   D. $39,000

6. What is the amount of the creditors' claims against the assets of the business?   6.____
   A. $4,000   B. $57,000   C. $32,000   D. $28,000

7. What is the net income for the period?   7.____
   A. $57,000
   B. $0
   C. $25,000
   D. This information cannot be obtained from the balance sheet

8. What was the value of Laura Lee's ownership in this business on January 1, 2004?   8.____
   A. $25,000
   B. $57,000
   C. $14,000
   D. This information cannot be obtained from the balance sheet

Questions 9-21.

DIRECTIONS: Each of the transactions described in Questions 9 through 21 occurred within an accounting period. For each question, indicate which of the four journals the transaction would be recorded in.

9. Sale of goods on account   9.___
    A. Cash receipts   B. Cash payments
    C. General   D. Sales

10. Cash payment of a promissory note   10.___
    A. Cash payments   B. Cash receipts
    C. Sales   D. General

11. Received a credit memo from a creditor   11.___
    A. Purchases   B. General
    C. Sales   D. Cash payments

12. Sale of merchandise for cash   12.___
    A. Purchases   B. General
    C. Cash receipts   D. Cash payments

13. Received a check from a customer in partial payment of   13.___
    an oral agreement
    A. Purchases   B. Sales
    C. General   D. Cash receipts

14. Issued a credit memo to a customer   14.___
    A. Purchases   B. General
    C. Cash payments   D. Sales

15. Received a promissory note in place of an oral agreement   15.___
    from a customer
    A. General   B. Cash payments
    C. Cash receipts   D. Sales

16. Paid monthly rent   16.___
    A. General   B. Purchases
    C. Cash payments   D. Cash receipts

17. Sale of a service on credit   17.___
    A. Cash receipts   B. General
    C. Purchases   D. Sales

18. Purchase of office furniture on credit   18.___
    A. General   B. Purchases
    C. Cash payments   D. Cash receipts

19. Purchased merchandise for cash   19.___
    A. Cash payments   B. Cash receipts
    C. Sales   D. General

20. Cash refund to a customer   20.___
    A. Cash receipts   B. Sales
    C. General   D. Cash payments

21. Purchases made on credit   21.___
    A. Purchases   B. Sales
    C. Cash receipts   D. General

Questions 22-26.

DIRECTIONS: Questions 22 through 26 are to be answered on the basis of the following inventory, purchased by International Soap and Candle Traders, Inc.

700 units at $4.50, 320 units at $3.75, 550 units at $2.75, and 475 units at $1.90

22. Calculate the total price of the units that cost $4.50.   22.____
    A. $315   B. $31,500   C. $3,150   D. $2,800

23. Calculate the total price of the units that cost $3.75.   23.____
    A. $2062.50   B. $12,000   C. $120   D. $1,200

24. Calculate the total price of the units that cost $2.75.   24.____
    A. $1,512.50   B. $15,125   C. $151.25   D. $550

25. Calculate the total price of the units that cost $1.90.   25.____
    A. $90.25   B. $9025   C. $902.50   D. $475

26. Calculate the average cost per unit.   26.____
    A. $27   B. $33.10   C. $0.30   D. $3.31

27. The interest on a promissory note is recorded at which   27.____
    of the following times?
    A. When the debt is incurred
    B. At the end of the accounting period
    C. When the note is paid
    D. At the beginning of each month

28. The interest on a promissory note begins accruing at   28.____
    which of the following times?
    A. When the debt is incurred
    B. At the end of the accounting period
    C. When the note is paid
    D. At the beginning of each month

29. The maturity value of an interest-bearing note is the   29.____
    A. interest accrued on the note plus a service charge
       imposed by the lender
    B. interest accrued on the note
    C. face value of the note
    D. principal of the note plus interest

30. A cash receipts journal is used to record the   30.____
    A. number of cash sales a business makes
    B. number of credit sales a business makes
    C. collection of cash made by the business
    D. expenditure of cash made by the business

31. Calculate the interest on a promissory note issued for
    $3,000 at an interest rate of 8%, due in 360 days.
    (Assume a banking year of 360 days.)
       A. $300   B. $240   C. $60   D. $360

31.____

32. Calculate the total payment due for a promissory note
    issued for $1,000 at an interest rate of 10%, due in
    90 days. (Assume a banking year of 360 days.)
       A. $25   B. $1050   C. $1000   D. $1025

32.____

33. Calculate the total payment due for a promissory note
    issued for $5,000 at an interest rate of 6%, due in 60
    days. (Assume a banking year of 360 days.)
       A. $5,050   B. $50   C. $5,000   D. $5,300

33.____

34. Calculate the interest on a promissory note issued for
    $1,700 at an interest rate of 12%, due in 45 days.
    (Assume a banking year of 360 days.)
       A. $204   B. $1725.50   C. $25.50   D. $1904

34.____

35. Calculate the interest on a promissory note issued for
    $600 at an interest rate of 9%, due in 90 days. (Assume
    a banking year of 360 days.)
       A. $13.50   B. $135   C. $54   D. $540

35.____

KEY (CORRECT ANSWERS)

1. B	11. B	21. A	31. B
2. C	12. C	22. C	32. D
3. A	13. D	23. D	33. A
4. B	14. B	24. A	34. C
5. B	15. A	25. C	35. A
6. C	16. C	26. D	
7. D	17. D	27. C	
8. D	18. B	28. A	
9. D	19. A	29. D	
10. A	20. D	30. C	

DIRECTIONS FOR THIS SECTION:
Solve the following accounting problems as directed. The problems must be solved arithmetically. Algebraic solutions are not acceptable.

TEST 1

PROBLEM

The following is a trial balance from the books of the County Medical Association as at July 1, 2004 and the balances on the books July 1, 2003.

	Trial Balance 7/1/04		Balance 7/1/03	
Cash	$ 20,552		$ 25,167	
Office Expense	4,825			
Library Expense	1,240			
Library	25,000		23,200	
Buildings	150,000		150,000	
Furniture	32,000		32,000	
Interest on Investments		4,100		
Investments	74,000		74,000	
Mortgage Payable		60,000		60,000
Interest on Mortgage	1,500			
Fines Levied		50		
Dues Receivable	12,000		2,700	
Dues Assessed 2004		21,600		
Salaries	7,200			
Publications	4,500			
Capital Surplus		247,067		247,067
	$332,817	$332,817	$307,067	$307,067

Each member was charged with dues individually in a dues ledger, and dues receivable in the general ledger is a controlling account.
The following data are to be noted:
- (a) Sundry expense items, as towel service, telephone service, etc., a total of $185, has not been charged to office expense.
- (b) Furniture is appraised as worth $30,000, July 1, 2004.
- (c) Interest has accrued on investment holdings for $375.
- (d) It is estimated that $1200 of the dues in arrears cannot be collected and should be written off.
- (e) Salaries of $155 are due and unpaid.
- (f) Publications for $1500 are to be carried over to next year. These publications are scientific papers for state distribution.
- (g) An outlay of $1800 was made for library books.

REQUIRED: With the above data prepare the statements of receipts and disbursements, income and expense, and the balance sheet.

SOLUTION

(a) COUNTY MEDICAL ASSOCIATION
Statement of Income and Expense
Year Ended July 1, 2004

Income:		
Dues Assessed	$21,600	
Interest on Investments	4,475	
Fines Levied	50	
Total Income		26,125

Expense:

Office Expense	5,010	
Library Expense	1,240	
Interest on Mortgage	1,500	
Salaries	7,355	
Publications	3,000	
Depreciation on Furniture	2,000	
Uncollectable Dues	1,200	
Total Expense		21,305
Net Income for Year		$ 4,820

(b) COUNTY MEDICAL ASSOCIATION
Statement of Receipts and Disbursements
Year Ended July 1, 2004

Cash Balance, July 1, 2003		$25,167
Receipts:		
Dues Collected	$12,300	
Interest on Investments	4,100	
Fines Levied	50	
Total Receipts		16,450
Total		$41,617
Disbursements:		
Library Books	1,800	
Office Expense	4,825	
Library Expense	1,240	
Interest on Mortgage	1,500	
Salaries	7,200	
Publications	4,500	
Total Disbursements		21,065
Cash Balance, July 1, 2004		$20,552

COMPUTATION OF DUES COLLECTED:

Dues Receivable, July 1, 2003	$ 2,700
Dues Assessed 2004	21,600
Total	24,300
Deduct: Dues Receivable, July 1, 2004	12,000
Dues Collected	12,300

(c) COUNTY MEDICAL ASSOCIATION
Balance Sheet
July 1, 2004

ASSETS:

Current:		
Cash	$20,552	
Dues Receivable	10,800	
Interest Accrued on Investments	375	
Total Current Assets		$31,727
Deferred Charges to Expense:		
Publication on Hand		1,500
Permanent Investments:		
Investments		74,000
Fixed:		
Furniture	30,000	
Library	25,000	
Buildings	150,000	
Total Fixed Assets		205,000
TOTAL ASSETS		$312,227

LIABILITIES AND CAPITAL:
   Current:
      Office Expense Payable $ 185
      Salaries Payable   155
         Total Current Liabilities   340
   Fixed:
      Mortgage Payable   60,000
        Total Liabilities   60,340
   Capital Surplus:
      Balance, July 1, 2003   247,067
      Add: Net Profit for Year   4,820
         Balance, July 1, 2004   251,887
         TOTAL LIABILITIES AND CAPITAL $312,227

It has been assumed that the Investments are not being held for current sale and have, therefore, been excluded from the Current Assets section.

TEST 2

PROBLEM

The European-American Machine Co. sells its product on 5 years' credit, payable in 5 equal annual installments. The cost of production for 2003 was $1,240,00; Sales, $1,550,000; General Expenses, $45,000. The year's installments were collected in full.

The sales for 2004 were $2,010,020; cost of production, $1,507,515; general expenses, $86,000. The regular installments due in 2004 were collected.

REQUIRED:(a) Write journal entries for the above.
         (b) Make a Profit and Loss Statement for each of the years 2003 and 2004.

SOLUTION

(a) Journal Entries for 2003

Accounts Receivable 2003	$1,550,000	
Installment Sales		$1,550,000
To record installment sales for 2003		
Cost of Goods Sold	1,240,000	
Finished Goods		1,240,000
To record cost of sales for 2003		
General Expenses	45,000	45,000
Cash		
To record expenses for 2003		
Cash	310,000	
Accounts Receivable 2003		310,000
To record collections for the year		
Installment Sales	1,550,000	
Cost of Goods Sold		1,240,000
Deferred Profits 2003		310,000
To close installment sales and set up the deferred profits for 2003		
Deferred Profits 2003	62,000	
Profit and Loss		62,000
To record profits realized, 20% of collections		

3

Profit and Loss	45,000	
General Expenses		45,000
To close		

Profit and Loss	17,000	
Surplus		17,000
To transfer net profit		

Journal Entries for 2004

Accounts Receivable 2004	$2,010,020	
Installment Sales		$2,010,020
To record installment sales for 2004		

Cost of Goods Sold	1,507,515	
Finished Goods		1,507,515
To record cost of sales for 2004		

General Expenses	86,000	
Cash		86,000
To record expenses for 2004		

Cash	712,004	
Accounts Receivable 2003		310,000
Accounts Receivable 2004		402,004
To record collections during 2004		

Installment Sales	2,010,020	
Cost of Goods Sold		1,507,515
Deferred Profits 2004		502,505
To close installment sales and set up deferred profits for 2004		

Deferred Profits 2003	62,000	
Deferred Profits 2004	100,501	
Profit and Loss		162,501
To record profits realized, 20% on 2003 collections and 25% on 2004 collections		

Profit and Loss	86,000	
General Expenses		86,000
To close		

Profit and Loss	76,501	
Surplus		76,501
To transfer net profit		

(b) EUROPEAN-AMERICAN MACHINE COMPANY
Profit and Loss Statement
Year Ended December 31, 2003

Installment Sales	$1,550,000
Cost of Goods Sold	1,240,000
Gross Profit	$ 310,000
Rate of Gross Profit	20%
Realized Gross Profit:	
Collections of $310,00 x 20%	62,000
General Expenses	45,000
Net Profit	$ 17,000

4

EUROPEAN-AMERICAN MACHINE COMPANY
Profit and Loss Statement
Year Ended December 31, 2004

Installment Sales		$2,010,020
Cost of Goods Sold		1,507,515
Gross Profit		$ 502,505
Rate of Gross Profit		**25%**
Realized Gross Profit:		
Acc. Rec. 2003 Collections $310,000x20%		62,000
Acc. Rec. 2004 Collections $402,004x25%		100,501
Total Realized Gross Profit		162,501
General Expenses		86,000
Net Profit	$	76,501

TEST 3

PROBLEM

The Pall Mall Company lost a part of its stock of merchandise by fire on the night of June 30, 2004. The merchandise was insured for $25,000 at a premium of $410 for one year, paid on Jan. 1. The policy contained the 80% standard co-insurance clause.

The following facts were ascertained: Inventory Jan. 1, $31,000; Purchases Jan. 1 to June 30, $116,000; Sales $160,000; Average gross profit for past three years 30% of sales; Inventory July 1, of goods not damaged by fire, $14,000.

REQUIRED: (a) What is the liability of the insurance company.
　　　　　(b) Write journal entries showing the amount and disposition of the fire loss and the unexpired insurance premium.

(a)　　　　　　　　　　　*SOLUTION*

COMPUTATION OF FIRE LOSS:

Sales	$160,000	
Gross Profit – 30% of Sales	48,000	
Cost of Goods Sold	$112,000	
Inventory, January 1, 2004		$ 31,000
Purchases, January 1 to June 30, 2004		116,000
Total		$147,000
Deduct: Cost of Goods Sold		112,000
Estimated Inventory, June 30, 2004		35,000
Deduct: Undamaged Inventory		14,000
Estimated Inventory Destroyed		$ 21,000

COMPUTATION OF LIABILITY OF INSURANCE COMPANY:

$$\text{Liability of Insurance Co.} = \frac{\text{Face of Policy}}{80\% \text{ of Value of Mdse. at Date of Loss}} \times \text{Loss}$$

$$= \frac{25,000}{80\% \ (35,000)} \times 21,000$$

$$= \frac{25,000}{28,000} \times 21,000$$

$$= 18,750$$

(b) Journal Entries
July 1, 2004

Fire Loss		$ 21,000	
Purchases			$ 21,000
To record fire loss			
Prepaid Insurance		205	
Insurance			205
To adjust insurance			
Cash		18,750	
Fire Loss			18,750
To record collection from insurance co.			
Fire Loss		153.75	
Prepaid Insurance			153.75

To charge to fire loss prepaid insurance
applicable to portion of policy cancelled
$$\frac{18,750}{25,000} \times 205 = 153.75$$

Dec. 31, 2004

Insurance Expense		51.25	
Prepaid Insurance			51.25
To adjust for expense of last 6 months			
Profit and Loss		256.25	
Insurance Expense			256.25
To close			
Surplus		2,403.75	
Fire Loss			2,403.75
To close			

TEST 4

PROBLEM

A and B, on winding up their partnership, found that their assets
realized as follows: Factory premises standing in their books at
$10,000 realized $4,000; Machinery standing in their books at $7,500
realized $2,500; Merchandise at $5,500 realized $4,350; Accounts Re-
ceivable of $9,500 realized $6,500; their unpaid liabilities were
$10,500. A's capital stood at $15,000, and B's capital at $7,000.
In respect of profit and losses they were equal partners. The liabilities were paid in full.

REQUIRED: Show how the partners' accounts stood after realization
and liquidation and show what each partner was entitled to
in order to settle the accounts.

SOLUTION

(a) SCHEDULE OF ASSETS REALIZED

	Book Value	Cash	Realization Loss
Factory	$10,000	$ 4,000	$ 6,000
Machinery	7,500	2,500	5,000
Merchandise	5,500	4,350	1,150
Accounts Receivable	9,500	6,500	3,000
	$32,500	$17,350	$15,150

6

(b) STATEMENT OF CAPITAL BALANCES

	A Capital	B Capital	Total
Balances before liquidation	$15,000	$ 7,000	$22,000
Realization loss, equally	7,575	7,575	15,150
Balance after liquidation	$ 7,425	$ 575*	$ 6,850

*Since B's capital account shows a debit balance of $575, it is obvious that the cash of $6,850, which remained from the $17,350 after paying off the liabilities of $10,500, should go to A. This would result in the following:

	A Capital	B Capital	Total
Balances, after liquidation	$ 7,425	$ 575*	$ 6,850
Cash to A	6,850	- - -	6,850
Balances	$ 575	$ 575	$ - - -

*A's capital account still shows a credit balance of $575; B's capital account shows a debit balance of the same amount. In other words, B owes A that amount.

If B does not pay the amount due and the books are to be closed, an entry may be made debiting A Capital and crediting B Capital for $575.

If B does pay the sum due, an entry may be made, debiting Cash and crediting B Capital for $575. This would be followed by an entry debiting A Capital and crediting Cash for the withdrawal of the cash by A. The books would then be closed.

TEST 5

PROBLEM

The following are the Balance Sheets of Company A and its subsidiary, Company B, as at December 31, 2000.

ASSETS	COMPANY A	COMPANY B
Plant and Equipment	$150,000	$ 50,000
Goodwill	90,000	15,000
Investment Co. B – Stock par value 75,000	85,000	
Inventories	100,000	60,000
Accounts Receivable	240,000	75,000
Cash	50,000	10,000
Notes Receivable of Co. B	20,000	
Dividends Receivable	3,000	
	$738,000	$210,000

LIABILITIES AND CAPITAL		
Notes Payable - to Co. A		20,000
Accounts Payable	200,000	80,000
Dividends Payable	10,000	4,000
Capital Stock	500,000	100,000
Surplus	28,000	6,000
	$738,000	$210,000

Company A owns 75% of the capital stock of Company B, which was acquired at the time of organization of Company B.
There are $10,000 of inter-company profits to be eliminated from inventories December 31, 2000.

REQUIRED: Prepare a working sheet and a consolidated balance sheet.

SOLUTION

(a) Company A and Company B
Working Sheet for Consolidated Balance Sheet
Dec. 31, 2000

ASSETS	CO. A	CO. B	ELIMINATIONS DR.	ELIMINATIONS CR.	CONSOLIDATED
Plant and Equipment	$150,000	50,000			$200,000
Goodwill	90,000	15,000	(d)10,000		115,000
Investment in Co. B	85,000			(d)85,000	
Inventories	100,000	60,000		(a)10,000	150,000
Accounts Receivable	240,000	75,000			315,000
Cash	50,000	10,000			60,000
Notes Receivable of Co. B	20,000			(b)20,000	
Dividends Receivable	3,000			(c) 3,000	
	$738,000	210,000			840,000
LIABILITIES AND CAPITAL					
Notes Payable to Co. A		20,000	(b)20,000		
Accounts Payable	200,000	80,000			280,000
Dividends Payable	10,000	4,000	(c) 3,000		11,000
Capital Stock-Co. A	500,000				500,000
Surplus - Co. A	28,000		(a)10,000		18,000
Capital Stock - Co. B					
Holding Co. Share		75,000	(d)75,000		
Minority Share		25,000			25,000
Surplus - Co. B					
Holding Co. Share		4,500			4,500
Minority Share		1,500			1,500
	$738,000	210,000			840,000

(b) Company A and Company B
Consolidated Balance Sheet
Dec. 31, 2000

ASSETS

Current:

Cash	$ 60,000	
Accounts Receivable	315,000	
Inventories	150,000	
Total Current Assets		$525,000

Fixed:

Plant and Equipment		200,000

Intangibles:

Goodwill		115,000
Total Assets		$840,000

LIABILITIES AND CAPITAL

Current:

Accounts Payable	$280,000	
Dividends Payable	11,000	
Total Liabilities	291,000	
Minority Interest in Co. B	26,500	
Capital Stock	$500,000	
Surplus	22,500	
Total Net Worth		522,500
Total Liabilities and Capital		$840,000

With regard to the elimination of the intercompany profit in the inventories, the wording of the problem has been accepted literally.

Thus, since it is specifically stated that $10,000 of intercompany profits "are to be eliminated," there has been no attempt to vary from the statement as given. If only the fact that there were $10,000 in intercompany profits in the inventories had been furnished, a different elimination figure might have been made.

TEST 6

PROBLEM

The following figures are taken from the books of the York Oil Pump Co.: Purchases of raw material, $42,400; direct labor, $37,800; inventory of finished pumps, Jan. 1, $16,700; factory expenses, $21,000; inventory of raw materials, Jan. 1, $6,500; cost of goods sold, $102,230; factory supplies, $6,100, of which $550 are still on hand; inventory of unfinished pumps, Jan. 1, $10,000, and on June 30, $12,500; selling expenses, $27,400; inventory of raw materials, June 30, $6,900; general expenses, $19,620; reserve for depreciation of machinery, $4,800; net sales $164,100. Depreciation of machinery for the period, $900.

REQUIRED: (a) Prepare a statement of Cost of Pumps manufactured during the six months January - June.
           (b) Compute inventory of pumps on hand June 30.

SOLUTION

(a) YORK OIL PUMP COMPANY
Statement of Cost of Pumps Manufactured
Six Months Ended June 30, 2003

Inventory of Raw Materials, Jan. 1		$ 6,500
Purchases of Raw Materials		42,400
Total Materials Available for Manufacture		48,900
Deduct: Raw Materials Inventory, June 30		6,900
Raw Materials Used		42,000
Direct Labor		37,800
Prime Cost		79,800
Factory Expenses:		
Factory Expenses	$21,000	
Depreciation of Machinery	900	
Factory Supplies Used	5,550	
Total Factory Expenses		27,450
Total Charges to Manufacturing		107,250
Add: Inventory Unfinished Pumps, Jan. 1		10,000
Total Available for Manufacture		117,250
Deduct: Inventory Unfinished Pumps, June 30		12,500
Cost of Pumps Manufactured		$104,750

(b) Computation of Finished Goods Inventory
June 30, 2003

Inventory Finished Pumps, Jan. 1	$ 16,700
Add: Cost of Pumps Manufactured	104,750
Total Pumps Available for Sale	$121,450
Deduct: Cost of Pumps Sold	102,230
Inventory Finished Pumps, June 30	$ 19,220

TEST 7

PROBLEM

Balance Sheet of the Chelsea Company, Dec. 31, 2004

1. Real Estate	$ 150,000	15. Common Stock	$1,000,000
2. Buildings	500,000	16. Pref. Stock (non-	
3. Accts. Receivable	80,000	participating)	500,000
4. Sinking Fund	45,000	17. Bonds	400,000
5. Treasury Stock (pref.)	75,000	18. Reserve for improvement	50,000
6. Discount on Bonds	60,000	19. Reserve for uncollect-	
7. Cash Reserves	23,000	able debts	5,000
8. Disc. on pref. stock	38,000	20. Res. for maintenance	6,000
9. Notes Receivable	30,000	21. Res. for taxes	13,000
10. Unissued com. stock	300,000	22. Res. for depreciation	18,000
11. Cash	75,000	23. Undivided profits	40,000
12. Equipment	250,000	24. Dividends payable	9,000
13. Inventories	450,000	25. Surplus	70,000
14. Prepaid items	50,000	26. Res. for Contingencies	9,000
		27. Accrued payables	6,000
	$2,126,000		$2,126,000

REQUIRED: In connection with the above balance sheet:
  (a) Give journal entries for the transactions giving rise to the following accounts: 4, 5, 7, 8, 14, and 18 to 27, inclusive.
  (b) Give journal entries for transactions which would result in the reduction or elimination of the balances in the following accounts: 5, 7, 10, 14, 16 and 18 to 27, inclusive.

SOLUTION

(a) 4. Sinking Fund
            Cash
     5. Treasury Stock
            Cash
         or Donated Surplus
     7. Cash Reserves
            Cash
     8. Cash
         Discount on Preferred Stock
            Unissued Preferred Stock
     14. Prepaid Items
            Expense Accounts
     18. Surplus or Undivided Profits
            Reserve for Improvement
     19. Bad Debts
            Reserve for uncollectable debts
     20. Maintenance
            Reserve for Maintenance
     21. Surplus or Undivided Profits
         or Taxes
            Reserve for Taxes
     22. Depreciation
            Reserve for Depreciation
     23. Profit and Loss
            Undivided Profits
     24. Surplus or Undivided Profits
            Dividends Payable

10

25. Undivided Profits
        Surplus
26. Surplus or Undivided Profits
        Res. for Contingencies
27. Expense Accounts
        Accrued Payables

(b) 5. Cash
        Donated Surplus
            Treasury Stock
7. Cash
        Cash Reserves
10. Cash
        Unissued Common Stock
14. Expense Accounts
        Prepaid items (on reversal)
16. Preferred Stock (Non-Participating)
        Surplus (on recapitalization)
18. Reserve for Improvements
        Undivided Profits, or Surplus
19. Reserve for Uncollectable Debts
        Accounts Receivable
20. Reserve for Maintenance
        Cash
21. Reserve for Taxes
        Cash
22. Reserve for Depreciation
        Buildings (on sale)
23. Undivided Profits
        Dividends Payable
    or Surplus
24. Dividends Payable
        Cash
25. Surplus
        Undivided Profits
26. Reserve for Contingencies
        Cash
27. Accrued Payables
        Expense Accounts (on reversal)
    or Cash

TEST 8

PROBLEM

On January 1, 1998, a corporation sold $200,000 of its ten-year First Mortgage 8% Bonds (semi-annual coupons) at 105.

REQUIRED: (a) Make entries for this transaction and for payment of interest on July 1, 1998 and Jan. 1, 1999. Show how the bond premium should be handled.

(b) Assuming that you are the purchaser of ten of the above bonds, write entries for their purchase and for the receipt of the two interest payments. Show how you would handle the bond premium upon your books.

SOLUTION

(a)
                    January 1, 1998

Cash $210,000

    First Mortgage Bonds Payable $200,000
    Premium on Bonds   10,000
Sold 10 year, 8% bonds at 105

                    July 1, 1998

Bond Interest Expense   8,000
    Cash   8,000
Paid semi-annual coupon due today
Premium on Bonds   500
    Bond Interest Expense   500
To amortize premium for 1/2 year

                December 31, 1998

Bond Interest Expense   8,000
    Bond Interest Expense Payable   8,000
To accrue interest for 1/2 year

Premium on Bonds   500
    Bond Interest Expense   500
To amortize for 1/2 year

Profit and Loss   15,000
    Bond Interest Expense   15,000
To close

                    January 1, 1999

Bond Interest Expense Payable   8,000
    Cash   8,000
Paid semi-annual coupon due today

It has been assumed that the books are closed each December 31. The unamortized portion of the Premium on Bonds account appears as a Deferred Credit in the Liability section on a classified balance sheet.

(b)
                    January 1, 1998

Bond Investment $ 10,500
    Cash $ 10,500
Purchased 10 First Mtge. 8% bonds at 105

                    July 1, 1998

Cash   400
    Bond Interest Income   400
Received semi-annual coupon due today

                    January 1, 1999

Cash   400
    Bond Interest Income   400
Received semi-annual coupon due today

Since amortization of bond premium on the purchaser's books is not recognized by the current income tax regulations, the solution above has ignored the recording of the premium and the amortization thereof.

Had the purchaser desired to show the premium, contrary to the tax regulations, the effect would have been to reduce the interest income by the amount of the resulting amortization. A separate Premium on Bon account could have been set up as a debit, classified as a Deferred Charge on a balance sheet, or the Bond Investment account could have been set up at cost, as in the above solution, and amortized over a ten year period to equal par value at maturity.

There has been no attempt to make either adjusting or closing entries due to insufficient information in the problem as presented.

TEST 9

PROBLEM

Comparative Balance Sheet of C. D. Company

Assets	Dec. 31, 2003	Dec. 31, 2004
Cash	$ 32,500	$ 12,100
Accounts Receivable	34,400	28,200
Bonds	1,300	27,300
Inventories	27,300	36,900
Plant	62,000	67,000
Machinery & Tools	99,000	102,000
Insurance	400	600
Goodwill	35,000	35,000
	$291,900	$309,100

Liabilities		
Capital Stock	$150,000	$150,000
Accounts Payable	51,200	16,100
Bonds Payable	2,000	18,000
Disc. on Bonds	500	1,500
Reserve for Depreciation	4,500	6,500
Surplus	83,700	117,000
	$291,900	$309,100

The profits for the year were $33,300. The directors desire a statement showing what has become of the cash and why they cannot declare a large dividend in view of the fact that they have made a considerable profit.

REQUIRED: Make a working sheet and prepare the statement desired.

SOLUTION

THE C. D. COMPANY
Application of Funds – Working Papers
Year Ended December 31, 2004

Assets	December 31, 2003	December 31, 2004	Year's Changes Dr.	Year's Changes Cr.
Cash	$ 32,500	$ 12,100	$	$20,400
Accounts Receivable	34,400	28,200		6,200
Bonds	1,300	27,300	26,000	
Inventories	27,300	36,900	9,600	
Plant	62,000	67,000	5,000	
Machinery and Tools	99,000	102,000	3,000	
Insurance	400	600	200	
Goodwill	35,000	35,000		
	$291,900	$309,100		
Liabilities				
Capital Stock	$150,000	$150,000		
Accounts Payable	51,200	16,100	35,100	
Bonds Payable	2,000	18,000		16,000
Discount on Bonds	500	1,500		1,000
Reserve for Depreciation	4,500	6,500		2,000
Surplus	83,700	117,000		33,300
	$291,900	$309,100	$78,900	$78,900

Funds Provided by Profits:
    Net Profit
    Depreciation for the year

Increase in Working Capital

THE C. D. COMPANY
Statement of Application of Funds
Year Ended December 31, 2004

Funds Provided:
  By Profits:
    Net Profit for the Year $33,300
    Add: Charges Not Requiring
      Funds:
      Depreciation   2,000 $35,300
  By Sale of Bonds   16,000
Total Funds Provided $51,300

Funds Applied:
  To Purchase of Bonds   25,000
  To Additions to Plant   5,000
  To Purchase of Mach. & Tools   3,000
  To Increase in Working Capital   18,300
Total Funds Applied $51,300

THE C. D. COMPANY
Application of Funds - Working Papers
Year Ended December 31, 2004

Adjustments Dr.	Adjustments Cr.	Working Increase	Capital Decrease	Funds Applied	Funds Provided
$	$	$	$ 20,400	$	$
			6,200		
	(c) 1,000			25,000	
		9,600			
				5,000	
				3,000	
		200			
		35,100			
					16,000
(c) 1,000					
(b) 2,000					
(a) 33,300					
	(a) 33,300				35,300
	(b) 2,000				
$36,300	$36,300	$44,900	$26,600		
			18,300	18,300	
		$44,900	$44,900	$51,300	$51,300

The Discount on Bonds, showing a credit balance, must represent discount on bonds purchased. Since no information is available regarding any amortization of this discount during 2004, none has been assumed. The increase of $1,000 has been tied up with the increase of $26,000 in the Bonds account so that an application of only $25,000 in cash for these additional bonds has resulted.

TEST 10

PROBLEM

The National Electric Co. supplies electric power and light to the City of Landow and to the local Street Railway Co. From the following figures, make out a statement of Revenues and Expenses and a Statement of Cash Receipts and Disbursements for the six months ending June 30, 2004.

Power sold to manufacturers, $123,500, of which $21,800 has not been collected; received from customers for electric light service, $87,200; due from customers on previous bills rendered, $6,100; bills for past month for light service amounting to $12,750 have not yet been rendered paid for operating expenses and salaries, $114,900, and $12,800; accrued repairs and maintenances amounted to $69,700, of which $10,400 is unpai new equipment was purchased for $35,000 but not yet paid for; received from Street Railway Co. for power, $64,000, and $10,900 is still due; cash balance on hand Jan. 1, $43,500.

SOLUTION

THE NATIONAL ELECTRIC COMPANY
Statement of Revenues and Expenses
Six Months Ended June 30, 2004

Sources of Revenue:		
Power Sold to Manufacturers	$123,500	
Power Sold to Street Railway Co.	74,900	
Electric Light Sold to Customers	99,950	
Total		$298,350
Expenses:		
Operating Expenses and Salaries	127,700	
Repairs and Maintenances	69,700	
Total		197,400
Net Income		$100,950

THE NATIONAL ELECTRIC COMPANY
Statement of Cash Receipts and Disbursements
Six Months Ended June 30, 2004

Cash Balance, Jan. 1, 2004		$ 43,500
Receipts:		
Power Sold to Manufacturers	$101,700	
Power Sold to Street Railway Co.	64,000	
Electric Light Sold to Customers	87,200	
Total Receipts		252,900
Total		$296,400
Disbursements:		
Operating Expenses and Salaries	114,900	
Repairs and Maintenance	59,300	
Total Disbursements		174,200
Cash Balance, June 30, 2004		$122,200

The item, due from customers on previous bills rendered, $6,100, is assumed to have been earned in a prior period and has been excluded from the current revenues. The new equipment purchased has likewise been ignored since it is neither an expense nor a disbursement of the period under consideration.

Problem

On April 1,2005,Barnes,of Trenton,New Jersey,ships an invoice of goods to Gray in New York. The goods are valued at $2,000,and the consignor pays freight amounting to $40, and insurance,$30. The consignee pays cartage amounting to $50, and storage,$40. On April 2, Barnes draws a 30-day draft against Gray for $500,which is duly accepted on April 5. The goods are sold for $2700. Gray's commission is 5%.

Draft the journal entries and set up the necessary accounts both on the books of the consignor and on those of the consignee to reflect the above transactions.

Solution
(a) Journal Entries on Consignor's Books
April 1,2005

Consignment Out,Gray	$2,000.00	
Purchases		$2,000.00
To record cost of goods shipped on consignment		
Consignment,Gray	70.00	
Cash		70.00
To record payments made on account of Goods con-		
signed to Gray, Freight $40, Insurance $30		
Notes Receivable	500.00	
Gray		500.00
To enter 30-day draft drawn on latter on 4/2 and		
accepted by him today		
Consignment Out, Gray	225.00	
Gray	2,475.00	
Consignment Out, Gray		2,700.00
To credit the consignment with its sales and		
charge it with its expenses as follows:		

        Cartage ....$ 50.00
        Storage 40.00
        5% Commission on $2,700 ...135.00 $225.00

Consignment Out, Gray	405.00	
Consignment Profit and Loss		405.00
To transfer the profit on this consignment		

(b) Journal Entires – Consignee's Books
April 1, 2005

Consignment (Memo)	2,000.00	
Consignments In, Barnes (Memo)		2,000.00
To set up memo accounts of the receipt of Barnes'		
goods		
Consignment In, Barnes	90.00	
Cash		90.00
Cartage $50 and Storage $40 paid on Barnes'goods		
Barnes, Principal	500.00	
Notes Payable		500.00
Accepted 30-day sight draft,date 4/2/05		
Accounts Receivable	2,700.00	
Consignments In,Barnes		2,700.00
To set up sales		
Consignments In, Barnes	135.00	
Commissions earned		135.00
To charge Barnes with commissions of 5% on Sales of $2,700		
Consignments In,Barnes (Memo)	2,000.00	
Consignments (Memo)		2,000.00
To reverse		
Consignments In,Barnes	2,475.00	
Barnes, Principal		2,475.00
To set amount due Barnes		

17

PREPARING WRITTEN MATERIAL

EXAMINATION SECTION

DIRECTIONS FOR TESTS 1-2:

Each of the sentences in the tests that follow may be classified under one of the following four categories:

A. *Faulty* because of incorrect grammar or sentence structure
B. *Faulty* because of incorrect punctuation
C. *Faulty* because of incorrect capitalization
D. *Correct*

Examine each sentence carefully to determine under which of the above four options it is best classified. Then, in the space on the right, print the capital letter preceding the option which is the *BEST* of the four suggested above.

(Each incorrect sentence contains but one type of error. Consider a sentence to be correct if it contains none of the types of errors mentioned, even though there may be other correct ways of expressing the same thought.)

TEST 1

1. This fact, together with those brought out at the previous meeting, prove that the schedule is satisfactory to the employees.   1. ...

2. Like many employees in scientific fields, the work of bookkeepers and accountants requires accuracy and neatness.   2. ...

3. "What can I do for you," the secretary asked as she motioned to the visitor to take a seat.   3. ...

4. Our representative, Mr. Charles will call on you next week to determine whether or not your claim has merit.   4. ...

5. We expect you to return in the spring; please do not disappoint us.   5. ...

6. Any supervisor, who disregards the just complaints of his subordinates, is remiss in the performance of his duty.   6. ...

7. Because she took less than an hour for lunch is no reason for permitting her to leave before five o'clock.   7. ...

8. "Miss Smith," said the supervisor, "Please arrange a meeting of the staff for two o'clock on Monday."   8. ...

9. A private company's vacation and sick leave allowance usually differs considerably from a public agency.   9. ...

10. Therefore, in order to increase the efficiency of operations in the department, a report on the recommended changes in procedures was presented to the departmental committee in charge of the program.   10. ...

11. We told him to assign the work to whoever was available.   11. ...

12. Since John was the most efficient of any other employee in the bureau, he received the highest service rating.   12. ...

13. Only those members of the national organization who resided in the middle West attended the conference in Chicago.   13. ...

14. The question of whether the office manager has as yet attained, or indeed can ever hope to secure professional status is one which has been discussed for years.   14. ...

15. No one knew who to blame for the error which, we later discovered, resulted in a considerable loss of time.   15. ...

TEST 2

1. The National alliance of Businessmen is trying to persuade private businesses to hire youth in the summertime.   1. ...

2. The supervisor who is on vacation, is in charge of pro-   2. ...
   cessing vouchers.
3. The activity of the committee at its conferences is al-   3. ...
   ways stimulating.
4. After checking the addresses again, the letters went to   4. ...
   the mailroom.
5. The director, as well as the employees, are interested   5. ...
   in sharing the dividends.

DIRECTIONS FOR TESTS 3 and 4: In each of the following groups of sentences, one of the four sentences is faulty in grammar, punctuation,
or capitalization. Select the incorrect sentence in each case.

TEST 3

1. A. Sailing down the bay was a thrilling experience for me.   6. ...
   B. He was not consulted about your joining the club.
   C. This story is different. than the one I told you yesterday.
   D. There is no doubt about his being the best player.
2. A. He maintains there is but one road to world peace.   7. ...
   B. It is common knowledge that a child sees much he is not
      supposed to see.
   C. Much of the bitterness might have been avoided if arbitra-
      tion had been resorted to earlier in the meeting.
   D. The man decided it would be advisable to marry a girl
      somewhat younger than him.
3. A. In this book, the incident I liked least is where the   8. ...
      hero tries to put out the forest fire.
   B. Learning a foreign language will undoubtedly give a
      person a better understanding of his mother tongue.
   C. His actions made us wonder what he planned to do next.
   D. Because of the war, we were unable to travel during the
      summer vacation.
4. A. The class had no sooner become interested in the lesson   9. ...
      than the dismissal bell rang.
   B. There is little agreement about the kind of world to be
      planned at the peace conference.
   C. "Today," said the teacher, "we shall read 'The Wind in
      the Willows.' I am sure you'll like it.
   D. The terms of the legal settlement of the family quarrel
      handicapped both sides for many years.
5. A. I was so suprised that I was not able to say a word.   10. ...
   B. She is taller than any other member of the class.
   C. It would be much more preferable if you were never seen
      in his company.
   D. We had no choice but to excuse her for being late.

2

TEST 4

1. A. Please send me these data at the earliest opportunity.   1. ...
   B. The loss of their material proved to be a severe handicap.
   C. My principal objection to this plan is that it is impracticable.
   D. The doll had laid in the rain for an hour and was ruined.

2. A. The garden scissors, left out all night in the rain,   2. ...
   were in a badly rusted condition.
   B. The girls felt bad about the misunderstanding which had arisen.
   C. Sitting near the campfire, the old man told John and I about many exciting adventures he had had.
   D. Neither of us is in a position to undertake a task of that magnitude.

3. A. The general concluded that one of the three roads would   3. ...
   lead to the besieged city.
   B. The children didn't, as a rule, do hardly anything beyond what they were told to do.
   C. The reason the girl gave for her negligence was that she had acted on the spur of the moment.
   D. The daffodils and tulips look beautiful in that blue vase.

4. A. If I was ten years older, I should be interested in   4. ...
   this work.
   B. Give the prize to whoever has drawn the best picture.
   C. When you have finished reading the book, take it back to the library.
   D. My drawing is as good as or better than yours.

5. A. He asked me whether the substance was animal or   5. ...
   vegetable.
   B. An apple which is unripe should not be eaten by a child.
   C. That was an insult to me who am your friend.
   D. Some spy must of reported the matter to the enemy.

6. A. Limited time makes quoting the entire message impossible.   6. ...
   B. Who did she say was going?
   C. The girls in your class have dressed more dolls this year than we.
   D. There was such a large amount of books on the floor that I couldn't find a place for my rocking chair.

7. A. What with his sleeplessness and his ill health, he was   7. ...
   unable to assume any responsibility for the success of the meeting.
   B. If I had been born in February, I should be celebrating my birthday soon.
   C. In order to prevent breakage, she placed a sheet of paper between each of the plates when she packed them.
   D. After the spring shower, the violets smelled very sweet.

8. A. He had laid the book down very reluctantly before the   8. ...
      end of the lesson.
   B. The dog, I am sorry to say, had lain on the bed all night.
   C. The cloth was first lain on a flat surface; then it was
      pressed with a hot iron.
   D. While we were in Florida, we lay in the sun until we
      were noticeably tanned.

9. A. If John was in New York during the recent holiday   9. ...
      season, I have no doubt he spent most of his time with
      his parents.
   B. How could he enjoy the television program; the dog was
      barking and the baby was crying.
   C. When the problem was explained to the class, he must have
      been asleep.
   D. She wished that her new dress were finished so that she
      could go to the party.

10. A. The engine not only furnishes power but light and heat 10.
       as well.
    B. You're aware that we've forgotten whose guilt was
       established, aren't you?
    C. Everybody knows that the woman made many sacrifices for
       her children.
    D. A man with his dog and gun is a familiar sight in this
       neighborhood.

TEST 5

DIRECTIONS FOR TEST 5:
   Each of Questions 1 to 15 consists of a sentence which may be
classified appropriately under one of the following four categories:
   A. *Incorrect* because of faulty grammar
   B. *Incorrect* because of faulty punctuation
   C. *Incorrect* because of faulty spelling
   D. *Correct*

Examine each sentence carefully. Then, print, in the space on the
right, the letter preceding the category which is the best of the four
suggested above.
   (Note: Each incorrect sentence contains only one type of error.
Consider a sentence correct if it contains no errors, although there
may be other correct ways of writing the sentence.)
1. Of the two employees, the one in our office is the most   1. ...
   efficient.
2. No one can apply or even understand, the new rules and   2. ...
   regulations.
3. A large amount of supplies were stored in the empty office.3. ...
4. If an employee is occassionally asked to work overtime,   4. ...
   he should do so willingly.
5. It is true that the new procedures are difficult to use   5. ...
   but, we are certain that you will learn them quickly.

6. The office manager said that he did not know who would be   6. ...
given a large allotment under the new plan.
7. It was at the supervisor's request that the clerk agreed   7. ...
to postpone his vacation.
8. We do not believe that it is necessary for both he and   8. ...
the clerk to attend the conference.
9. All employees, who display perseverance, will be given   9. ...
adequate recognition.
10. He regrets that some of us employees are dissatisfied   10. ...
with our new assignments.
11. Do you think that the raise was merited," asked the   11. ...
supervisor?
12. The new manual of procedure is a valuable supplament to   12. ...
our rules and regulations.
13. The typist admitted that she had attempted to pursuade   13. ...
the other employees to assist her in her work.
14. The supervisor asked that all amendments to the regula-   14. ...
tions be handled by you and I.
15. The custodian seen the boy who broke the window.   15. ...

KEYS (CORRECT ANSWERS)

TEST 1		TEST 2		TEST 3		TEST 4		TEST 5	
1.	A	1.	C	1.	C	1.	D	1.	A
2.	A	2.	B	2.	D	2.	C	2.	B
3.	B	3.	D	3.	A	3.	B	3.	A
4.	B	4.	A	4.	C	4.	A	4.	C
5.	D	5.	A	5.	C	5.	D	5.	B
6.	B					6.	D	6.	D
7.	A					7.	B	7.	D
8.	C					8.	C	8.	A
9.	A					9.	B	9.	B
10.	D					10.	A	10.	D
11.	D							11.	B
12.	A							12.	C
13.	C							13.	C
14.	B							14.	A
15.	A							15.	A

PREPARING WRITTEN MATERIAL

PARAGRAPH REARRANGEMENT
COMMENTARY

The sentences which follow are in scrambled order. You are to rearrange them in proper order and indicate the letter choice containing the correct answer at the space at the right.

Each group of sentences in this section is actually a paragraph presented in scrambled order. Each sentence in the group has a place in that paragraph; no sentence is to be left out. You are to read each group of sentences and decide upon the best order in which to put the sentences so as to form as well-organized paragraph.

The questions in this section measure the ability to solve a problem when all the facts relevant to its solution are not given.

More specifically, certain positions of responsibility and authority require the employee to discover connections between events sometimes, apparently, unrelated. In order to do this, the employee will find it necessary to correctly infer that unspecified events have probably occurred or are likely to occur. This ability becomes especially important when action must be taken on incomplete information.

Accordingly, these questions require competitors to choose among several suggested alternatives, each of which presents a different sequential arrangement of the events. Competitors must choose the MOST logical of the suggested sequences.

In order to do so, they may be required to draw on general knowledge to infer missing concepts or events that are essential to sequencing the given events. Competitors should be careful to infer only what is essential to the sequence. The plausibility of the wrong alternatives will always require the inclusion of unlikely events or of additional chains of events which are NOT essential to sequencing the given events.

It's very important to remember that you are looking for the best of the four possible choices, and that the best choice of all may not even be one of the answers you're given to choose from.

There is no one right way to these problems. Many people have found it helpful to first write out the order of the sentences, as they would have arranged them, on their scrap paper before looking at the possible answers. If their optimum answer is there, this can save them some time. If it isn't, this method can still give insight into solving the problem. Others find it most helpful to just go through each of the possible choices, contrasting each as they go along. You should use whatever method feels comfortable, and works, for you.

While most of these types of questions are not that difficult, we've added a higher percentage of the difficult type, just to give you more practice. Usually there are only one or two questions on this section that contain such subtle distinctions that you're unable to answer confidently, and you then may find yourself stuck deciding between two possible choices, neither of which you're sure about.

EXAMINATION SECTION
TEST 1

DIRECTIONS: The sentences that follow are in scrambled order. You are to rearrange them in proper order and indicate the letter choice containing the correct answer. *PRINT THE LETTER OF THE CORRECT ANSWER IN THE SPACE AT THE RIGHT.*

1. Below are four statements labeled W., X., Y., and Z.   1.____
    W.   He was a strict and fanatic drillmaster.
    X.   The word is always used in a derogatory sense and generally shows resentment and anger on the part of the user.
    Y.   It is from the name of this Frenchman that we derive our English word, martinet.
    Z.   Jean Martinet was the Inspector-General of Infantry during the reign of King Louis XIV.
    The *PROPER* order in which these sentences should be placed in a paragraph is:

    A. X, Z, W, Y   B. X, Z, Y, W   C. Z, W, Y, X   D. Z, Y, W, X

2. In the following paragraph, the sentences which are numbered, have been jumbled.   2.____
    1.   Since then it has undergone changes.
    2.   It was incorporated in 1955 under the laws of the State of New York.
    3.   Its primary purpose, a cleaner city, has, however, remained the same.
    4.   The Citizens Committee works in cooperation with the Mayor's Inter-departmental Committee for a Clean City.
    The order in which these sentences should be arranged to form a well-organized paragraph is:

    A. 2, 4, 1, 3   B. 3, 4, 1, 2   C. 4, 2, 1, 3   D. 4, 3, 2, 1

Questions 3-5.

DIRECTIONS: The sentences listed below are part of a meaningful paragraph but they are not given in their proper order. You are to decide what would be the *best order* in which to put the sentences so as to form a well-organized paragraph. Each sentence has a place in the paragraph; there are no extra sentences. You are then to answer questions 3 to 5 inclusive on the basis of your rearrangements of these secrambled sentences into a properly organized paragraph.

In 1887 some insurance companies organized an Inspection Department to advise their clients on all phases of fire prevention and protection. Probably this has been due to the smaller annual fire losses in Great Britain than in the United States. It tests various fire prevention devices and appliances and determines manufacturing hazards and their safeguards. Fire research began earlier in the United States and is more advanced than in Great Britain. Later they established a laboratory specializing in electrical, mechanical, hydraulic, and chemical fields.

3. When the five sentences are arranged in proper order, the paragraph starts with the sentence which begins

    3.____

    A. "In 1887..."   B. "Probably this ..."   C. "It tests ..."
    D. "Fire research ..."   E. "Later they ..."

4. In the last sentence listed above, "they" refers to

    4.____

    A. insurance companies
    B. the United States and Great Britain
    C. the Inspection Department
    D. clients
    E. technicians

5. When the above paragraph is properly arranged, it ends with the words

    5.____

    A. "... and protection."   B. "... the United States."
    C. "... their safeguards."   D. "... in Great Britain."
    E. "... chemical fields."

KEY (CORRECT ANSWERS)

    1. C
    2. C
    3. D
    4. A
    5. C

TEST 2

DIRECTIONS: In each of the questions numbered 1 through 5, several sentences are given. For each question, choose as your answer the group of numbers that represents the *most logical* order of these sentences if they were arranged in paragraph form. *PRINT THE LETTER OF THE CORRECT ANSWER IN THE SPACE AT THE RIGHT.*

1. 1. It is established when one shows that the landlord has prevented the tenant's enjoyment of his interest in the property leased.
   2. Constructive eviction is the result of a breach of the covenant of quiet enjoyment implied in all leases.
   3. In some parts of the United States, it is not complete until the tenant vacates within a reasonable time.
   4. Generally, the acts must be of such serious and permanent character as to deny the tenant the enjoyment of his possessing rights.
   5. In this event, upon abandonment of the premises, the tenant's liability for that ceases.

   The CORRECT answer is:

   A. 2, 1, 4, 3, 5   B. 5, 2, 3, 1, 4   C. 4, 3, 1, 2, 5
   D. 1, 3, 5, 4, 2

   1._____

2. 1. The powerlessness before private and public authorities that is the typical experience of the slum tenant is reminiscent of the situation of blue-collar workers all through the nineteenth century.
   2. Similarly, in recent years, this chapter of history has been reopened by anti-poverty groups which have attempted to organize slum tenants to enable them to bargain collectively with their landlords about the conditions of their tenancies.
   3. It is familiar history that many of the workers remedied their condition by joining together and presenting their demands collectively.
   4. Like the workers, tenants are forced by the conditions of modern life into substantial dependence on these who possess great political arid economic power.
   5. What's more, the very fact of dependence coupled with an absence of education and self-confidence makes them hesitant and unable to stand up for what they need from those in power.

   The CORRECT answer is:

   A. 5, 4, 1, 2, 3   B. 2, 3, 1, 5, 4   C. 3, 1, 5, 4, 2
   D. 1, 4, 5, 3, 2

   2._____

3. 1. A railroad, for example, when not acting as a common carrier may contract; away responsibility for its own negligence.
   2. As to a landlord, however, no decision has been found relating to the legal effect of a clause shifting the statutory duty of repair to the tenant.
   3. The courts have not passed on the validity of clauses relieving the landlord of this duty and liability.
   4. They have, however, upheld the validity of exculpatory clauses in other types of contracts.
   5. Housing regulations impose a duty upon the landlord to maintain leased premises in safe condition.

   3._____

6. As another example, a bailee may limit his liability except for gross negligence, willful acts, or fraud.

The CORRECT answer is:

A. 2, 1, 6, 4, 3, 5 B. 1, 3, 4, 5, 6, 2 C. 3, 5, 1, 4, 2, 6
D. 5, 3, 4, 1, 6, 2

4. 1. Since there are only samples in the building, retail or consumer sales are generally 4._____
eschewed by mart occupants, and,in some instances, rigid controls are maintained
to limit entrance to the mart only to those persons engaged in retailing.
 2. Since World War I, in many larger cities, there has developed a new type of
property, called the mart building.
 3. It can, therefore, be used by wholesalers and jobbers for the display of sample
merchandise.
 4. This type of building is most frequently a multi-storied, finished interior property
which is a cross between a retail arcade and a loft building.
 5. This limitation enables the mart occupants to ship the orders from another location after the retailer or dealer makes his selection from the samples.

The CORRECT answer is:

A. 2, 4, 3, 1, 5 B. 4, 3, 5, 1, 2 C. 1, 3, 2, 4, 5
D. 1, 4, 2, 3, 5

5. 1. In general, staff-line friction reduces the distinctive contribution of staff personnel. 5._____
 2. The conflicts, however, introduce an uncontrolled element into the managerial
system.
 3. On the other hand, the natural resistance of the line to staff innovations probably
usefully restrains over-eager efforts to apply untested procedures on a large
scale.
 4. Under such conditions, it is difficult to know when valuable ideas are being sacri-
ficed.
 5. The relatively weak position of staff, requiring accommodation to the line, tends
to restrict their ability to engage .in free, experimental innovation.

The CORRECT answer is:

A. 4, 2, 3, 1, 3 B. 1, 5, 3, 2, 4 C. 5, 3, 1, 2, 4
D. 2, 1, 4, 5, 3

KEY (CORRECT ANSWERS)

1. A
2. D
3. D
4. A
5. B

TEST 3

DIRECTIONS: Questions 1 through 4 consist of six sentences which can be arranged in a logical sequence. For each question, select the choice which places the numbered sentences in the *most logical* sequence. *PRINT THE LETTER OF THE CORRECT ANSWER IN THE SPACE AT THE RIGHT.*

1. 1. The burden of proof as to each issue is determined before trial and remains upon the same party throughout the trial.   1._____
    2. The jury is at liberty to believe one witness' testimony as against a number of contradictory witnesses.
    3. In a civil case, the party bearing the burden of proof is required to prove his contention by a fair preponderance of the evidence.
    4. However, it must be noted that a fair preponderance of evidence does not necessarily mean a greater number of witnesses.
    5. The burden of proof is the burden which rests upon one of the parties to an action to persuade the trier of the facts, generally the jury, that a proposition he asserts is true.
    6. If the evidence is equally balanced, or if it leaves the jury in such doubt as to be unable to decide the controversy either way, judgment must be given against the party upon whom the burden of proof rests.

    The CORRECT answer is:

    A. 3, 2, 5, 4, 1, 6   B. 1, 2, 6, 5, 3, 4   C. 3, 4, 5, 1, 2, 6
    D. 5, 1, 3, 6, 4, 2

2. 1. If a parent is without assets and is unemployed, he cannot be convicted of the crime of non-support of a child.   2._____
    2. The term "sufficient ability" has been held to mean sufficient financial ability.
    3. It does not matter if his unemployment is by choice or unavoidable circumstances.
    4. If he fails to take any steps at all, he may be liable to prosecution for endangering the welfare of a child.
    5. Under the penal law, a parent is responsible for the support of his minor child only if the parent is "of sufficient ability."
    6. An indigent parent may meet his obligation by borrowing money or by seeking aid under the provisions of the Social Welfare Law.

    The CORRECT answer is:

    A. 6, 1, 5, 3, 2, 4   B. 1, 3, 5, 2, 4, 6   C. 5, 2, 1, 3, 6, 4
    D. 1, 6, 4, 5, 2, 3

3. 1. Consider, for example, the case of a rabble rouser who urges a group of twenty people to go out and break the windows of a nearby factory.
    2. Therefore, the law fills the indicated gap with the crime of inciting to riot."
    3. A person is considered guilty of inciting to riot when he urges ten or more persons to engage in tumultuous and violent conduct of a kind likely to create public alarm.
    4. However, if he has not obtained the cooperation of at least four people, he cannot be charged with unlawful assembly.
    5. The charge of inciting to riot was added to the law to cover types of conduct which cannot be classified as either the crime of "riot" or the crime of "unlawful assembly."
    6. If he acquires the acquiescence of at least four of them, he is guilty of unlawful assembly even if the project does not materialize.

    The CORRECT answer is:

    A. 3, 5, 1, 6, 4, 2   B. 5, 1, 4, 6, 2, 3   C. 3, 4, 1, 5, 2, 6
    D. 5, 1, 4, 6, 3, 2

3.___

4. 1. If, however, the rebuttal evidence presents an issue of credibility, it is for the jury to determine whether the presumption has, in fact, been destroyed.
    2. Once sufficient evidence to the contrary is introduced, the presumption disappears from the trial.
    3. The effect of a presumption is to place the burden upon the adversary to come forward with evidence to rebut the presumption.
    4. When a presumption is overcome and ceases to exist in the case, the fact or facts which gave rise to the presumption still remain.
    5. Whether a presumption has been overcome is ordinarily a question for the court.
    6. Such information may furnish a basis for a logical inference.

    The CORRECT answer is:

    A. 4, 6, 2, 5, 1, 3   B. 3, 2, 5, 1, 4, 6   C. 5, 3, 6, 4, 2, 1
    D. 5, 4, 1, 2, 6, 3

4.___

————

KEY (CORRECT ANSWERS)

1. D
2. C
3. A
4. B

————

BASIC FUNDAMENTALS OF A FINANCIAL STATEMENT

TABLE OF CONTENTS

BASIC FUNDAMENTALS
OF A FINANCIAL STATEMENT

COMMENTARY

The ability to read and understand a financial statement is a basic requirement for the accountant, auditor, account clerk, bookkeeper, bank examiner. budget examiner, and, of course, for the executive who must manage and administer departmental affairs.

FINANCIAL REPORTS

Are financial reports really as difficult as all that? Well, if you know they are not so difficult because you have worked with them before, this section will be of auxiliary help for you. However, if you find financial statements a bit murky, but realize their great importance to you, we ought to get along fine together. For "mathematics," all we'll use is fourth-grade arithmetic.

Accountants, like all other professionals, have developed a specialized vocabulary. Sometimes this is helpful and sometimes plain confusing (like their practice of calling the income account, "Statement of Profit and Loss," when it is bound to be one or the other). But there are really only a score or so technical terms that you will have to get straight in mind. After that is done, the whole foggy business will begin to clear and in no time at all you'll be able to talk as wisely as the next fellow.

BALANCE SHEET

Look at the sample balance sheet printed on page 2, and we'll have an insight into how it is put together. This particular report is neither the simplest that could be issued, nor the most complicated. It is a good average sample of the kind of report issued by an up-to-date manufacturing company.

Note particularly that the *balance sheet* represents the situation as it stood on one particular day, December 31, not the record of a year's operation. This balance sheet is broken into two parts: on the left are shown *ASSETS* and on the right *LIABILITIES*. Under the asset column, you will find listed the value of things the company owns or are owed to the company. Under liabilities, are listed the things the company owes to others, plus reserves, surplus, and the stated value of the stockholders' interest in the company.

One frequently hears the comment, "Well, I don't see what a good balance sheet is anyway, because the assets and liabilities are always the same whether the company is successful or not."

It is true that they always balance and, by itself, a balance sheet doesn't tell much until it is analyzed. Fortunately, we can make a balance sheet tell its story without too much effort -- often an extremely revealing story, particularly, if we compare the records of several years. ASSETS The first notation on the asset side of the balance sheet is *CURRENT* ASSETS (item 1). In general, current assets include cash and things that can be turned into cash in a hurry, or that, in the normal course of business, will be turned into cash in the reasonably near future, usually within a year.

Item 2 on our sample sheet is *CASH*. Cash is just what you would expect -bills and silver in the till and money on deposit in the bank.

UNITED STATES GOVERNMENT SECURITIES is item 3. The general practice is to show securities listed as current assets at cost or market value, whichever is lower. The figure, for all reasonable purposes, represents the amount by which total cash could be easily increased if the company wanted to sell these securities.

The next entry is *ACCOUNTS RECEIVABLE* (item 4). Here we find the total amount of money owed to the company by its regular business creditors and collectable within the next year. Most of the money is owed to the company by its customers for goods that the company delivered on credit. If this were a department store instead of a manufacturer, what you owed the store on your charge account would be included here. Because some people fail to pay their bills, the company sets up a reserve for doubtful accounts, which it subtracts from all the money owed.

THE ABC MANUFACTURING COMPANY, INC.
CONSOLIDATED BALANCE SHEET – DECEMBER 31

Item				
1. CURRENT ASSETS				
2. Cash				
3. U.S. Government Securities				
4. Accounts Receivable (less reserves)	2,000,000			
5. Inventories (at lower of cost or market)	2,000,000			
6. Total Current Assets	$7,000,000			
7. INVESTMENT IN AFFIL-IATED COMPANY Not consolidated (at cost, not in ex-cess of net assets)	200,000			
8. OTHER INVESTMENTS At cost, less than market	100,000			
9. PLANT IMPROVEMENT FUND	550,000			
10. PROPERTY, PLANT AND EQUIPMENT:				
Cost	$8,000,000			
11. Less Reserve for Deprecia-tion	5,000,000			
12. NET PROPERTY	3,000,000			
13. PREPAYMENTS	50,000			
14. DEFERRED CHARGES	100,000			
15. PATENTS AND GOODWILL	100,000			

Item			
16. CURRENT LIABILITIES			
17. Accts. Payable	$ 300,000		
18. Accrued Taxes	800,000		
19. Accrued Wages, Interest and Other Expenses	370,000		
20. Total Current Liabilities	$1,470,000		
21. FIRST MORTGAGE SINK-ING FUND BONDS, 3 1/2% DUE 2002	2,000,000		
22. RESERVE FOR CON-TINGENCIES	200,000		
23. CAPITAL STOCK:			
24. 5% Preferred Stock (author-ized and issued 10,000 shares of $100 par value)	$1,000,000		
25. Common stock (author-ized and issued 400,000 shares of no par value)	1,000,000	2,000,000	
26. SURPLUS:			
27. Earned	3,530,000		
28. Capital (arising from sale of common capital stock at price in excess of stated value)	1,900,000	5,430,000	

TOTAL	$11,100,000

TOTAL	$11,100,000

2

Item 5, *INVENTORIES,* is the value the company places on the supplies it owns. The inventory of a manufacturer may contain raw materials that it uses in making the things it sells, partially finished goods in process of manufacture and, finally, completed merchandise that it is ready to sell. Several methods are used to arrive at the value placed on these various items. The most common is to value them at their cost or present market value, whichever is lower. You can be reasonably confident, however, that the figure given is an honest and significant one for the particular industry if the report is certified by a reputable firm of public accountants.

Next on the asset side is *TOTAL CURRENT ASSETS* (item 6). This is an extremely important figure when used in connection with other items in the report, which we will come to presently. Then we will discover how to make total current assets tell their story.

INVESTMENT IN AFFILIATED COMPANY (item 7) represents the cost to our parent company of the capital stock of its *subsidiary* or affiliated company. A subsidiary is simply one company that is controlled by another. Most corporations that own other companies outright, lump the figures in a *CONSOLIDATED BALANCE SHEET.* This means that, under cash, for example, one would find a total figure that represented *all* of the cash of the parent company and of its wholly owned subsidiary. This is a perfectly reasonable procedure because, in the last analysis, all of the money is controlled by the same persons.

Our typical company shows that it has *OTHER INVESTMENTS* (item 8), in addition to its affiliated company. Sometimes good marketable securities other than Government bonds are carried as current assets, but the more conservative practice is to list these other security holdings separately. If they have been bought as a permanent investment, they would always be shown by themselves. "At cost, less than market" means that our company paid $100,000 for these other investments, but they are now worth more.

Among our assets is a *PLANT IMPROVEMENT FUND* (item 9). Of course, this item does not appear in all company balance sheets, but is typical of *special funds* that companies set up for one purpose or another. For example, money set aside to pay off part of the bonded debt of a company might be segregated into a special fund. The money our directors have put aside to improve the plant would often be invested in Government bonds.

FIXED ASSETS

The next item (10), is *PROPERTY, PLANT AND EQUIPMENT,* but it might just as well be labeled *Fixed Assets* as these terms are used more or less interchangeably. Under item 10, the report gives the value of land, buildings, and machinery and such movable things as trucks, furniture, and hand tools. Historically, probably more sins were committed against this balance sheet item than any other.

In olden days, cattlemen used to drive their stock to market in the city. It was a common trick to stop outside of town, spread out some salt for the cattle to make them thirsty and then let them drink all the water they could hold. When they were weighed for sale, the cattlemen would collect cash for the water the stock had drunk. Business buccaneers, taking the cue from their farmer friends, would often "write up" the value of their fixed assets. In other words, they would increase the value shown on the balance sheet, making the capital stock appear to be worth a lot more than it was. *Watered stock* proved a bad investment for most stockholders. The practice has, fortunately, been stopped, though it took major financial reorganizations to squeeze the water out of some securities.

The most common practice today is to list fixed assets at cost. Often, there is no ready market for most of the things that fall under this heading, so it is not possible to give market value. A good report will tell what is included under fixed assets and how it has been valued. If the value has been increased by *write-up* or decreased by *write-down,* a footnote explanation is usually given. A *write-up* might occur, for instance, if the value of real estate increased substantially. A *write-down* might follow the invention of a new machine that put an important part of the company's equipment out of date.

DEPRECIATION

Naturally, all of the fixed property of a company will wear out in time (except, of course, non-agricultural land). In recognition of this fact, companies set up a *RESERVE FOR DEPRECIATION* (item 11). If a truck costs $4,000 and is expected to last four years, it will be depreciated at the rate of $1,000 a year.

Two other terms also frequently occur in connection with depreciation -*depletion* and *obsolescence.* Companies may lump depreciation, depletion, and obsolescence under a single title, or list them separately.

Depletion is a term used primarily by mining and oil companies (or any of the so-called extractive industries). Depletion means exhaust or use up. As the oil or other natural resource is used up, a reserve is set up, to compensate for the natural wealth the company no longer owns. This reserve is set up in recognition of the fact that, as the company sells its natural product, it must get back not only the cost of extracting but also the original cost of the natural resource.

Obsolescence represents the loss in value because a piece of property has gone out of date before it wore out. Airplanes are modern examples of assets that tend to get behind the times long before the parts wear out. (Women and husbands will be familiar with the speed at which ladies' hats "obsolesce.")

In our sample balance sheet we have placed the reserve for depreciation under fixed assets and then subtracted, giving us *NET PROPERTY* (item 12), which we add into the asset column. Sometimes, companies put the reserve for depreciation in the liability column. As you can see, the effect is just the same whether it is *subtracted* from assets or *added* to liabilities.

The manufacturer, whose balance sheet we use, rents a New York showroom and pays his rent yearly, in advance. Consequently, he has listed under assets *PREPAYMENTS* (item 13). This is listed as an asset because he has paid for the use of the showroom, but has not yet received the benefit from its use. The use is something coming to the firm in the following year and, hence, is an asset. The dollar value of this asset will decrease by one-twelfth each month during the coming year.

DEFERRED CHARGES (item 14) represents a type of expenditure similar to prepayment. For example, our manufacturer brought out a new product last year, spending $100,000 introducing it to the market. As the benefit from this expenditure will be returned over months or even years to come, the manufacturer did not think it reasonable to charge the full expenditure against costs during the year. He has *deferred* the charges and will write them off gradually.

INTANGIBLES

The last entry in our asset column is *PATENTS AND GOODWILL* (item 15). If our company were a young one, set up to manufacture some new patented prod uct, it would probably carry its patents at a substantial figure. In fact, *intangibles* of both old and new companies are often of great but generally unmeasurable worth.

Company practice varies considerably in assigning value to intangibles. Procter & Gamble, despite the tremendous goodwill that has been built up for IVORY SOAP, has reduced all of its intangibles to the nominal $1. Some of the big cigarette companies, on the contrary, place a high dollar value on the goodwill their brand names enjoy. Companies that spend a good deal for research and the development of new products are more inclined than others to reflect this fact in the value assigned to patents, license agreements, etc.

4

LIABILITIES

The liability side of the balance sheet appears a little deceptive at first glance. Several of the entries simply don't sound like liabilities by any ordinary definition of the term.

The first term on the liability side of any balance sheet is usually *CURRENT LIABILITIES* (item 16). This is a companion to the *Current Assets* item across the page and includes all debts that fall due within the next year. The relation between current assets and current liabilities is one of the most revealing things to be gotten from the balance sheet, but we will go into that quite thoroughly later on.

ACCOUNTS PAYABLE (item 17) represents the money that the company owes to its ordinary business creditors -- unpaid bills for materials, supplies, insurance, and the like. Many companies itemize the money they owe in a much more detailed fashion than we have done, but, as you will see, the totals are the most interesting thing to us.

Item 18, *ACCRUED TAXES,* is the tax bill that the company estimates it still owes for the past year. We have lumped all taxes in our balance sheet, as many companies do. However, sometimes you will find each type of tax given separately. If the detailed procedure is followed, the description of the tax is usually quite sufficient to identify the separate items.

Accounts Payable was defined as the money the company owed to its regular business creditors. The company also owes, on any given day, wages to its own employees; interest to its bondholders and to banks from which it may have borrowed money; fees to its attorneys; pensions, etc. These are all totaled under *ACCRUED WAGES, INTEREST AND OTHER EXPENSES* (item 19).

TOTAL CURRENT LIABILITIES (item 20) is just the sum of everything that the company owed on December 31 and which must be paid sometime in the next twelve months.

It is quite clear that all of the things discussed above are liabilities. The rest of the entries on the liability side of the balance sheet, however, do not seem at first glance to be liabilities.

Our balance sheet shows that the company, on December 31, had $2,000,000 of 3 1/2 percent First Mortgage *BONDS* outstanding (item 21). Legally, the money received by a company when it sells bonds is considered a loan to the company. Therefore, it is obvious that the company owes to the bondholders an amount equal to the face value or the *call price* of the bonds it has outstanding. The call price is a figure usually larger than the face value of the bonds at which price the company can *call* the bonds in from the bondholders and pay them off before they ordinarily fall due. The date that often occurs as part of the name of a bond is the date at which the company has promised to pay off the loan from the bondholders.

RESERVES

The next heading, *RESERVE FOR CONTINGENCIES* (item 22), sounds more like an asset than a liability. "My reserves," you might say, "are dollars in the bank, and dollars in the bank are assets."

No one would deny that you have something there. In fact, the corporation treasurer also has his reserve for contingencies balanced by either cash or some kind of unspecified investment on the asset side of the ledger. His reason for setting up a reserve on the liability side of the balance sheet is a precaution against making his financial position seem better than it is. He decided that the company might have to pay out this money during the coming year if certain things happened. If he did not set up the "reserve," his surplus would appear larger by an amount equal to his reserve.

A very large reserve for contingencies or a sharp increase in this figure from the previous year should be examined closely by the investor. Often, in the past, companies tried to hide their true earnings by transferring funds into a contingency reserve. As a reserve looks somewhat like a true liability, stockholders were confused about the real value of their securities. When a reserve is not set up for protection against some very probable loss or expenditure, it should be considered by the investor as part of surplus.

CAPITAL STOCK

Below reserves there is a major heading, *CAPITAL STOCK* (item 23). Companies may have one type of security outstanding, or they may have a dozen. All of the issues that represent shares of ownership are capital, regardless of what they are called on the balance sheet -- preferred stock, preference stock, common stock, founders' shares, capital stock, or something else.

Our typical company has one issue of 5 per cent *PREFERRED STOCK* (item 24). It is called *preferred* because those who own it have a right to dividends and assets before the *common* stockholders -- that is, the holders are in a preferred position as owners. Usually, preferred stockholders do not have a voice in company affairs unless the company fails to pay them dividends at the promised rate. Their rights to dividends are almost always *cumulative*. This simply means that all past dividends must be paid before the other stockholders can receive anything. Preferred stockholders are not creditors of the company so it cannot properly be said that the company *owes* them the value of their holdings. However, in case the company decided to go out of business, preferred stockholders would have a prior claim on anything that was left in the company treasury after all of the creditors, including the bondholders, were paid off. In practice, this right does not always mean much, but it does explain why the book value of their holdings is carried as a liability.

COMMON STOCK (item 25) is simple enough as far as definition is concerned it represents the rights of the ordinary owner of the company. Each company has as many owners as it has stockholders. The proportion of the company that each stockholder owns is determined by the number of shares he has. However, neither the book value of a no-par common stock, nor the par value of an issue that has a given par, can be considered as representing either the original sale price, the market value, or what would be left for the stockholders if the company were liquidated.

A profitable company will seldom be dissolved. Once things have taken such a turn that dissolution appears desirable, the stated value of the stock is generally nothing but a fiction. Even if the company is profitable as a going institution, once it ceases to function even its tangible assets drop in value because there is not usually a ready market for its inventory of raw materials and semi-finished goods, or its plant and machinery.

SURPLUS

The last major heading on the liability side of the balance sheet is *SURPLUS* (item 26). The surplus, of course, is not a liability in the popular sense at all. It represents, on our balance sheet, the difference between the stated value of our common stock and the net assets behind the stock.

Two different kinds of surplus frequently appear on company balance sheets, and our company has both kinds. The first type listed is *EARNED* surplus (item 27). Earned surplus is roughly similar to your own savings. To the corporation, earned surplus is that part of net income which has not been paid to stockholders as dividends. It still *belongs* to you, but the directors have decided that it is best for the company and the stockholders to keep it in the business. The surplus may be invested in the plant just as you might invest part of your savings in your home. It may also be in cash or securities.

In addition to the earned surplus, our company also has a *CAPITAL* surplus (item 28) of $1,900.00, which the balance sheet explains arose from selling the stock at a higher cost per share than is given as its stated value. A little arithmetic shows that the stock is carried on the books at $2.50 a share while the capital surplus amounts to $4.75 a share. From this we know that the company actually received an average of $7.25 net a share for the stock when it was sold.

WHAT DOES THE BALANCE SHEET SHOW?

Before we undertake to analyze the balance sheet figures, a word on just what an investor can expect to learn is in order. A generation or more ago, before present accounting standards had gained wide acceptance, considerable imagination went into the preparation of balance sheets. This, naturally, made the public skeptical of financial reports. Today, there is no substantial ground for skepticism. The certified public accountant, the listing requirements of the national stock exchanges, and the regulations of the Securities and Exchange Commission have, for all practical purposes, removed the grounds for doubting the good faith of financial reports.

The investor, however, is still faced with the task of determining the significance of the figures. As we have already seen, a number of items are based, to a large degree, upon estimates, while others are, of necessity, somewhat arbitrary.

NET WORKING CAPITAL

There is one very important thing that we can find from the balance sheet and accept with the full confidence that we know what we are dealing with. That is net working capital, sometimes simply called working capital.

On the asset side of our balance sheet we have added up all of the current assets and show the total as item 6. On the liability side, item 20 gives the total of current liabilities. *Net working capital* or *net current assets* is the difference left after subtracting current liabilities from current assets. If you consider yourself an investor rather than a speculator, you should always insist that any company in which you invest have a comfortable amount of working capital. The ability of a company to meet its obligations with ease, expand its volume as business expands and take advantage of opportunities as they present themselves, is, to an important degree, determined by its working capital.

Probably the question in your mind is: *"Just what does 'comfortable amount' of working capital mean?"* Well, there are several methods used by analysts to judge whether a particular company has a sound working capital position. The first rough test for an industrial company is to compare the working capital figure with the current liability total. Most analysts say that minimum safety requires that net working capital at least equal current liabilities. Or, put another way, that current assets should be at least twice as large as current liabilities.

There are so many different kinds of companies, however, that this test requires a great deal of modification if it is to be really helpful in analyzing companies in different industries. To help you interpret the *current position* of a company in which you are considering investing, the *current ratio* is more helpful than the dollar total of working capital. The current ratio is current assets divided by current liabilities.

In addition to working capital and current ratio, there are two other ways of testing the adequacy of the current position. *Net quick assets* provide a rigorous and important test of a company's ability to meet its current obligations. Net quick assets are found by taking total current assets (item 6) and subtracting the value of inventories (item 5). A well-fixed industrial company should show a reasonable excess of quick assets over current liabilities..

Finally, many analysts say that a good industrial company should have at least as much working capital (current assets less current liabilities) as the total book value of its bonds and preferred stock. In other words, current liabilities, bonded debt, and preferred stock *altogether* should not exceed the current assets.

INVENTORY AND INVENTORY TURNOVER

In the recent past, there has been much talk of inventories. Many commentators have said that these carry a serious danger to company earnings if management allows them to increase too much. Of course, this has always been true, but present high prices have made everyone more inventory-conscious than usual.

There are several dangers in a large inventory position. In the first place, a sharp drop in price may cause serious losses; also, a large inventory may indicate that the company has accumulated a big supply of unsalable merchandise. The question still remains, however: *"What do we mean by large inventory?"*

As you certainly realize, an inventory is large or small only in terms of the yearly turnover and the type of business. We can discover the annual turnover of our sample company by dividing inventories (item 5) into total annual sales (item "a" on the income account).

It is also interesting to compare the value of the inventory of a company being studied with total current assets. Again, however, there is considerable variation between different types of companies, so that the relationship becomes significant only when compared with similar companies.

NET BOOK VALUE OF SECURITIES

There is one other very important thing that can be gotten from the balance sheet, and that is the net book or equity value of the company's securities. We can calculate the net book value of each of the three types of securities our company has outstanding by a little very simple arithmetic. *Book value means the value at which something is carried on the books of the company.*

The full rights of the bondholders come before any of the rights of the stockholders, so, to find the net book value or net tangible assets backing up the bonds we add together the balance sheet value of the bonds, preferred stock, common stock, reserve, and surplus. This gives us a total of $9,630,000. (We would not include contingency reserve if we were reasonably sure the contingency was going to arise, but, as general reserves are often equivalent to surplus, it is, usually, best to treat the reserve just as though it were surplus.) However, part of this value represents the goodwill and patents carried at $100,000, which is not a tangible item, so, to be conservative, we subtract this amount, leaving $9,530,000 as the total net book value of the bonds. This is equivalent to $4,765 for each $1,000 bond, a generous figure. To calculate the net book value of the preferred stock, we must eliminate the face value of the bonds, and then, following the same procedure, add the value of the preferred stock, common stock, reserve, and surplus, and subtract goodwill. This gives us a total net book value for the preferred stock of $7,530,000 or $753 for each share of $100 par value preferred. This is also very good coverage for the preferred stock, but we must examine current earnings before becoming too enthusiastic about the *value* of any security.

The net book value of the common stock, while an interesting figure, is not so important as the coverage on the senior securities. In case of liquidation, there is seldom much left for the common stockholders because of the normal loss in value of company assets when they are put up for sale, as mentioned before. The book value figure, however, does give us a basis for comparison with other companies. Comparisons of net book value over a period of years also show us if the company is a soundly growing one or, on the other hand, is losing ground. Earnings, however, are our important measure of common stock values, as we will see shortly.

The net book value of the common stock is found by adding the stated value of the common stock, reserves, and surplus and then subtracting patents and goodwill. This gives us a total net book value of $6,530,000. As there are 400,000 shares of common outstanding, each share has a net book value of $16.32. You must be careful not to be misled by book value figures, particularly of common stock. Profitable companies (Coca-Cola, for example) often show a very low net book value and very substantial earnings. Railroads, on the other hand, may show a high book value for their common stock but have such low or irregular earnings that the market price of the stock is much less than its apparent book value. Banks, insurance companies, and investment -trusts are exceptions to what we have said about common stock net book value. As their assets are largely liquid (i.e., cash, accounts receivable, and marketable securities), the book value of their common stock sometimes indicates its value very accurately.

PROPORTION OF BONDS, PREFERRED AND COMMON STOCK

Before investing, you will want to know the proportion of each kind of security issued by the company you are considering. A high proportion of bonds reduces the attractiveness of both the preferred and common stock, while too large an amount of preferred detracts from the value of the common.

The *bond ratio* is found by dividing the face value of the bonds (item 21), or $2,000,000, by the total value of the bonds, preferred stock, common stock, reserve, and surplus, or $9,630,000. This shows that bonds amount to about 20 per cent of the total of bonds, capital, and surplus.

The *preferred stock ratio* is found in the same way, only we divide the stated value of the preferred stock by the total of the other five items. Since we have half as much preferred stock as we have bonds, the preferred ratio is roughly 10.

Naturally, the *common stock ratio* will be the difference between 100 per cent and the totals of the bonds and preferred, or 70 per cent in our sample company. You will want to remember that the most valuable method of determining the common stock ratio is in combination with reserve and surplus. The surplus, as we have noted, is additional backing for the common stock and usually represents either original funds paid in to the company in excess of the stated value of the common stock (capital surplus), or undistributed earnings (earned surplus).

Most investment analysts carefully examine industrial companies that have more than about a quarter of their capitalization represented by bonds, while common stock should total at least as much as all senior securities (bonds and preferred issues). When this is not the case, companies often find it difficult to raise new capital. Banks don't like to lend them money because of the already large debt, and it is sometimes difficult to sell common stock because of all the bond interest or preferred dividends that must be paid before anything is available for the common stockholder.

Railroads and public utility companies are exceptions to most of the rules of thumb that we use in discussing The ABC Manufacturing Company, Inc. Their situation is different because of the tremendous amounts of money they have invested in their fixed assets., their small inventories and the ease with which they can collect their receivables. Senior securities of railroads and utility companies frequently amount to more than half of their capitalization. Speculators often interest themselves in companies that have a high proportion of debt or preferred stock because of the *leverage factor.* A simple illustration will show why. Let us take, for example, a company with $10,000,000 of 4 per cent bonds outstanding. If the company is earning $440,000 before bond interest, there will be only $40,000 left for the common stock ($10,000,000 at 4% equals $400,000). However, an increase of only 10 per cent in earnings (to $484,000) will leave $84,000 for common stock dividends, or an increase of more than 100 per cent. If there is only a small common issue, the increase in earnings per share would appear very impressive.

You have probably already noticed that a decline of 10 per cent in earnings would not only wipe out everything available for the common stock, but result in the company being unable to cover its full interest on its bonds without dipping into surplus. This is the great danger of so-called high leverage stocks and also illustrates the fundamental weakness of companies that have a disproportionate amount of debt or preferred stock. Investors would do well to steer clear of them. Speculators, however, will continue to be fascinated by the market opportunities they offer.

THE INCOME ACCOUNT

The fundamental soundness of a company, as shown by its balance sheet, is important to investors, but of even greater interest is the record of its operation. Its financial structure shows much of its ability to weather storms and pick up speed when times are good. It is the income record, however, that shows us how a company is actually doing and gives us our best guide to the future.

The *Consolidated Income and Earned Surplus* account of our company is stated on the next page. Follow the items given there and we will find out just how our company earned its money, what it did with its earnings, and what it all means in terms of our three classes of securities. We have used a combined income and surplus account because that is the form most frequently followed by industrial companies. However, sometimes the two statements are given separately. Also, a variety of names are used to describe this same part of the financial report. Sometimes it is called profit and loss account, sometimes *record of earnings,* and, often, simply *income account.* They are all the same thing.

The details that you will find on different income statements also vary a great deal. Some companies show only eight or ten separate items, while others will give a page or more of closely spaced entries that break down each individual type of revenue or cost. We have tried to strike a balance between extremes; give the major items that are in most income statements, omitting details that are only interesting to the expert analyst.

The most important source of revenue always makes up the first item on the income statement. In our company, it is *Net Sales* (item "a"). If it were a railroad or a utility instead of a manufacturer, this item would be called *gross revenues.* In any case, it represents the money paid into the company by its customers. Net sales are given to show that the figure represents the amount of money actually received after allowing for discounts and returned goods.

Net sales or gross revenues, you will note, is given before any kind of miscellaneous revenue that might have been received from investments, the sale of company property, tax refunds, or the like. A well-prepared income statement is always set up this way so that the stockholder can estimate the success of the company in fulfilling its major job of selling goods or service. If this were not so, you could not tell whether the company was really losing or making money on its operations, particularly over the last few years when tax rebates and other unusual things have often had great influence on final net income figures.

COST OF SALES

A general heading, *Cost of Sales, Expenses and Other Operating Charges* (item "b") is characteristic of a manufacturing company, but a utility company or railroad would call all of these things *operating expenses.*

The most important subdivision is *Cost of Goods Sold* (item "c"). Included under cost of goods sold are all of the expenses that go directly into the manufacture of the products the company sells -- raw materials, wages, freight, power, and rent. We have lumped these expenses together, as many companies do. Sometimes, however, you will find each item listed separately. Analyzing a detailed income account is a pretty technical operation and had best be left to the expert.

The ABC Manufacturing Company, Inc.
CONSOLIDATED INCOME AND EARNED SURPLUS
For the Year Ended December 31

Item

a.	Sales		$10,000,000
b.	COST OF SALES, EXPENSES AND OTHER OPERATING CHARGES:		
c.	Cost of Goods Sold	$7,000,000	
d.	Selling, Administrative & Gen. Expenses	500,000	
e.	Depreciation	200,000	
f.	Maintenance and Repairs	400,000	
g.	Taxes (Other than Federal Inc. Taxes)	300,000	8,400,000
h.	NET PROFIT FROM OPERATIONS		$ 1,600,000
i.	OTHER INCOME:		
j.	Royalties and Dividends	$ 250,000	
k.	Interest	25,000	275,000
l.	TOTAL		$ 1,875,000
m.	INTEREST CHARGES:		
n.	Interest on Funded Debt	$ 70,000	
o.	Other Interest	20,000	90,000
p.	NET INCOME BEFORE PROVISION FOR FED. INCOME TAXES		$ 1,785,000
q.	PROVISION FOR FEDERAL INCOME TAXES		678,300
r.	NET INCOME		$ 1,106,700
s.	DIVIDENDS:		
t.	Preferred Stock - $5.00 Per Share	$ 50,000	
u.	Common Stock - $1.00 Per Share	400,000	
v.	PROVISION FOR CONTINGENCIES	200,000	650,000
w.	BALANCE CARRIED TO EARNED SURPLUS		$ 456,700
x.	EARNED SURPLUS – JANUARY 1		3,073,000
y.	EARNED SURPLUS – DECEMBER 31		$ 3,530,000

We have shown separately, opposite "d," the *Selling, Administrative and General Expenses* of the past year. Unfortunately, there is little uniformity among companies in their treatment of these important non-manufacturing costs. Our figure includes the expenses of management; that is, executive salaries and clerical costs; commissions and salaries paid to salesmen; advertising expenses, and the like.

Depreciation ("e") shows us the amount that the company transferred from income during the year to the depreciation reserve that we ran across before as item "11" on the balance sheet (page 2). Depreciation must be charged against income unless the company is going to live on its own fat, something that no company can do for long and stay out of bankruptcy.

MAINTENANCE

Maintenance and Repairs (item "f") represents the money spent to keep the plant in good operating order. For example, the truck that we mentioned under depreciation must be kept running day by day. The cost of new tires, recharging the battery, painting and mechanical repairs are all maintenance costs. Despite this day-to-day work on the truck, the company must still provide for the time when it wears out -- hence, the reserve for depreciation.

You can readily understand from your own experience the close connection between maintenance and depreciation. If you do not take good care of your own car, you will have to buy a new one sooner than you would had you maintained it well. Corporations face the same problem with all of their equipment. If they do not do a good job of maintenance, much more will have to be set aside for depreciation to replace the abused tools and property.

Taxes are always with us. A profitable company always pays at least two types of taxes. One group of taxes are paid without regard to profits, and include real estate taxes, excise taxes, social security, and the like (item "g"). As these payments are a direct part of the cost of doing business, they must be included before we can determine the *Net Profit From Operations* (item "h").

Net Profit from Operations (sometimes called *gross profit)* tells us what the company made from manufacturing and selling its products. It is an interesting figure to investors because it indicates .how efficiently and successfully the company operates in its primary purpose as a creator of wealth. As a glance at the income account will tell you, there are still several other items to be deducted before the stockholder can hope to get anything. You can also easily imagine that for many companies these other items may spell the difference between profit and loss. For these reasons, we use net profit from operations as an indicator of progress in manufacturing and merchandising efficiency, not as a judge of the investment quality of securities.

Miscellaneous Income not connected with the major purpose of the company is generally listed after net profit from operations. There are quite a number of ways that corporations increase their income, including interest and dividends on securities they own, fees for special services performed, royalties on patents they allow others to use, and tax refunds. Our income statement shows *Other Income* as item "i," under which is shown income from *Royalties and Dividends* (item "j"), and, as a separate entry, *Interest* (item "k") which the company received from its bond investments. The *Total* of other income (item t1t?) shows us how much The ABC Manufacturing Company received from so-called *outside activities.* Corporations with diversified interests often receive tremendous amounts of *other income.*

INTEREST CHARGES

There is one other class of expenses that must be deducted from our income before we can determine the base on which taxes are paid, and that is *Interest Charges* (item "m"). As our company has $2,000,000 worth of 3 1/2 per cent bonds outstanding, it will pay *Interest on Funded Debt* of $70,000 (item "n"). During the year, the company also borrowed money from the bank, on which it, of course, paid interest, shown as *Other Interest* (item "o").

Net Income Before Provision for Federal Income Taxes (item "p") is an interesting figure for historical comparison. It shows us how profitable the company was in all of its various operations. A comparison of this entry over a period of years will enable you to see how well the company had been doing as a business institution before the Government stepped in for its share of net earnings. Federal taxes have varied so much in recent years that earnings before taxes are often a real help in judging business progress.

A few paragraphs back we mentioned that a profitable corporation pays two general types of taxes. We have already discussed those that are paid without reference to profits. *Provision for Federal Income Taxes* (item "q") is ordinarily figured on the total income of the company after normal business expenses, and so appears on our income account below these charges. Bond interest, for example, as it is payment on a loan, is deducted beforehand. Preferred and common stock dividends, which are *profits* that go to owners of the company, come after all charges and taxes.

NET INCOME

After we have deducted all of our expenses and income taxes from total income, we get *Net Income* (item "r"). Net income is the most interesting figure of all to the investor. Net income is the amount available to pay dividends on the preferred and common stock. From the balance sheet, we have learned a good deal about the company's stability and soundness of structure; from net profit from operations, we judge whether the company is improving in industrial efficiency. Net income tells us whether the securities of the company are likely to be a profitable investment.

The figure given for a single year is not nearly all of the story, however. As we have noted before, the historical record is usually more important than the figure for any given year. This is just as true of net income as any other item. So many things change from year to year that care must be taken not to draw hasty conclusions. During the war, Excess Profits Taxes had a tremendous effect on the earnings of many companies. In the next few years, *carryback tax credits* allowed some companies to show a net profit despite the fact that they had operated at a loss. Even net income can be a misleading figure unless one examines it carefully. A rough and easy way of judging how *sound* a figure it is would be to compare it with previous years.

The investor in stocks has a vital interest in *Dividends* (item "s"). The first dividend that our company must pay is that on its *Preferred Stock* (item "t"). Some companies will even pay preferred dividends out of earned surplus accumulated in the past if the net income is not large enough, but such a company is skating on thin ice unless the situation is most unusual.

The directors of our company decided to pay dividends totaling $400,000 on the *Common Stock,* or $1 a share (item "u"). As we have noted before, the amount of dividends paid is not determined by net income, but by a decision of the stockholders' representatives - the company's directors. Common dividends, just like preferred dividends, can be paid out of surplus if there is little or no net income. Sometimes companies do this if they have a long history of regular payments and don't want to spoil the record because of some special temporary situation that caused them to lose money. This occurs even less frequently and is more *dangerous* than paying preferred dividends out of surplus.

It is much more common, on the contrary, to *plough earnings back into the business* -- a phrase you frequently see on the financial pages and in company reports. The directors of our typical company have decided to pay only $1 on the common stock, though net income would have permitted them to pay much more. They decided that the company should *save* the difference.

The next entry on our income account, *Provision for Contingencies* (item "v"), shows us where our reserve for contingencies arose. The treasurer of our typical company has put the provision for contingencies after dividends. However, you will discover, if you look at very many financial reports, that it is sometimes placed above net income.

All of the net income that was not paid out as dividends, or set aside for contingencies, is shown as *Balance Carried to Earned Surplus* (item "w"). In other words, it is kept in the business. In previous years, the company had also earned more than it paid out so it had already accumulated by the beginning of the year an earned surplus of $3,073,000 (item "x"). When we total the earned surplus accumulated during the year to that which the company had at the first of the year, we get the total earned surplus at the end' of the year (item "y"). You will notice that the total here is the same as that which we ran across on the balance sheet as item 27.

Not all companies combine their income and surplus account. When they do not, you will find that *balance carried to surplus will* be the last item on the income account. The statement of consolidated surplus would appear as a third section of the corporation's financial report. A separate surplus account might be used if the company shifted funds for reserves to surplus during the year or made any other major changes in its method of treating the surplus account.

ANALYZING THE INCOME ACCOUNT

The income account, like the balance sheet, will tell us a lot more if we make a few detailed comparisons. The size of the totals on an income account doesn't mean much by itself. A company can have hundreds of millions of dollars in net sales and be a very bad investment. On the other hand, even a very modest profit in round figures may make a security attractive if there are only a small number of shares outstanding.

Before you select a company for investment, you will want to know something of its *margin of profit,* and how this figure has changed over the years. Finding the margin of profit is very simple. We just divide the net profit from operations (item "h") by net sales (item "a"). The figure we get (0.16) shows us that the company make a profit of 16 per cent from operations. By itself, though, this is not very helpful. We can make it significant in two ways.

In the first place, we can compare it with the margin of profit in previous years, and, from this comparison, learn if the company excels other companies that do a similar type of business. If the margin of profit of our company is very low in comparison with other companies in the same field, it is an unhealthy sign. Naturally, if it is high, we have grounds to be optimistic.

Analysts also frequently use *operating ratio* for the same purpose. The operating ratio is the complement of the margin of profit. The margin of profit of our typical company is 16. The operating ratio is 84. You can find the operating ratio either by subtracting the margin of profit from 100 or dividing the total of operating costs ($8,400,000) by net sales ($10,000,000).

The margin of profit figure and the operating ratio, like all of those ratios we examined in connection with the balance sheet, give us general information about the company, help us judge its prospects for the future. All of these comparisons have significance for the long term as they tell us about the fundamental economic condition of the company. But you still have the right to ask: *"Are the securities good investments for me now?"*

Investors, as opposed to speculators, are primarily interested in two things. The first is safety for their capital and the second, regularity of income. They are also interested in the rate of return on their investment but, as you will see, the rate of return will be affected by the importance placed on safety and regularity. High income implies risk. Safety must be bought by accepting a lower return.

The safety of any security is determined primarily by the earnings of the company that are available to pay interest or dividends on the particular issue. Again, though, round dollar figures aren't of much help to us. What we want to know is the relationship between the total money available and the requirements for each of the securities issued by the company.

INTEREST COVERAGE

As the bonds of our company represent part of its debt, the first thing we want to know is how easily the company can pay the interest. From the income account we see that the company had total income of $1,875,000 (item "1"). The interest charge on our bonds each year is $70,000 (3 1/2 per cent of $2,000,000 - item 21 on the balance sheet). Dividing total income by bond interest charges ($1,875,000 by $70,000) shows us that the company earned its bond interest 26 times over. Even after income taxes, bond interest was earned 17 times, a method of testing employed by conservative analysts. Before an industrial bond should be considered a safe investment, most analysts say that the company should earn interest charges several times over, so our company has a wide margin of safety.

To calculate the *preferred dividend coverage* (i.e., the number of times preferred dividends were earned), we must use net income as our base, as Federal Income Taxes and all interest charges must be paid before anything is available for stockholders. As we have 10,000 shares of $100 par value of preferred stock which pays a dividend of 5 per cent, the total dividend requirement for the preferred stock is $50,000 (items 24 on the balance sheet and "t" on the income account).

EARNINGS PER COMMON SHARE

The buyer of common stocks is often more concerned with the earnings per share of his stock than he is with the dividend. It is usually earnings per share or, rather, prospective earnings per share, that influence stock market prices. Our income account does not show the earnings available for the common stock, so we must calculate it ourselves. It is net income less preferred dividends (items "r" - "t"), or $1,056,700. From the balance sheet, we know that there are 400,000 shares outstanding, so the company earned about $2.64 per share.

All of these ratios have been calculated for a single year. It cannot be emphasized too strongly, however, that the *record* is more important to the investor than the report of any single year. By all the tests we have employed, both the bonds and the preferred stock of our typical company appear to be very good investments,, if their market prices were not too high. The investor would want to look back, however, to determine whether the operations were reasonably typical of the company.

Bonds and preferred stocks that are very safe usually sell at pretty high prices, so the yield to the investor is small. For example, if our company has been showing about the same coverage on its preferred dividends for many years and there is good reason to believe that the future will be equally kind, the company would probably replace the old 5 per cent preferred with a new issue paying a lower rate, perhaps 4 per cent.

STOCK PRICES

As the common stock does not receive a guaranteed dividend, its market value is determined by a great variety of influences in addition to the present yield of the stock measured by its dividends. The stock market, by bringing together buyers and sellers from all over the world, reflects their composite judgment of the present and future value of the stock. We cannot attempt here to write a treatise on the stock market. There is one important ratio, however, that every common stock buyer considers. That is the ratio of earnings to market price.

The so-called *price-earnings ratio is* simply the earnings per share on the common stock divided into the market price. Our typical company earned $2.64 a common share in the year, If the stock were selling at $30 a share, its price-earnings ratio would be about 11.4. This is the basic figure that you would want to use in comparing the common stock of this particular company with other similar stocks.

IMPORTANT TERMS AND CONCEPTS

LIABILITIES
> WHAT THE COMPANY OWES -- + RESERVES + SURPLUS + STOCKHOLDERS INTEREST IN THE COMPANY

ASSETS
> WHAT THE COMPANY OWNS -- + WHAT IS OWED TO THE COMPANY

FIXED ASSETS
> MACHINERY, EQUIPMENT, BUILDINGS, ETC.

EXAMPLES OF FIXED ASSETS
> DESKS, TABLES, FILING CABINETS, BUILDINGS, LAND, TIMBERLAND, CARS AND TRUCKS, LOCOMOTIVES AND FREIGHT CARS, SHIPYARDS, OIL LANDS, ORE DEPOSITS, FOUNDRIES

EXAMPLES OF:
> PREPAID EXPENSES
> > PREPAID INSURANCE, PREPAID RENT, PREPAID ROYALTIES AND PREPAID INTEREST

> DEFERRED CHARGES
> > AMORTIZATION OF BOND DISCOUNT, ORGANIZATION EXPENSE, MOVING EXPENSES, DEVELOPMENT EXPENSES

ACCOUNTS PAYABLE
> BILLS THE COMPANY OWES TO OTHERS

BONDHOLDERS ARE CREDITORS
> BOND CERTIFICATES ARE IOU'S ISSUED BY A COMPANY BACKED BY A PLEDGE

BONDHOLDERS ARE OWNERS
> A STOCK CERTIFICATE IS EVIDENCE OF THE SHAREHOLDER'S OWNERSHIP

EARNED SURPLUS
> INCOME PLOWED BACK INTO THE BUSINESS

NET SALES
> GROSS SALES MINUS DISCOUNTS AND RETURNED GOODS

NET INCOME
> = TOTAL INCOME MINUS ALL EXPENSES AND INCOME TAXES

ANSWER SHEET

EST NO. _____ PART _____ TITLE OF POSITION _____

(AS GIVEN IN EXAMINATION ANNOUNCEMENT - INCLUDE OPTION, IF ANY)

LACE OF EXAMINATION _____ DATE _____

(CITY OR TOWN)   (STATE)

RATING

USE THE SPECIAL PENCIL.   MAKE GLOSSY BLACK MARKS.

	A	B	C	D	E			A	B	C	D	E			A	B	C	D	E			A	B	C	D	E			A	B	C	D	E
1							26							51							76							101					
2							27							52							77							102					
3							28							53							78							103					
4							29							54							79							104					
5							30							55							80							105					
6							31							56							81							106					
7							32							57							82							107					
8							33							58							83							108					
9							34							59							84							109					
10							35							60							85							110					

Make only ONE mark for each answer.   Additional and stray marks may be counted as mistakes.   In making corrections, erase errors COMPLETELY.

	A	B	C	D	E			A	B	C	D	E			A	B	C	D	E			A	B	C	D	E			A	B	C	D	E
11							36							61							86							111					
12							37							62							87							112					
13							38							63							88							113					
14							39							64							89							114					
15							40							65							90							115					
16							41							66							91							116					
17							42							67							92							117					
18							43							68							93							118					
19							44							69							94							119					
20							45							70							95							120					
21							46							71							96							121					
22							47							72							97							122					
23							48							73							98							123					
24							49							74							99							124					
25							50							75							100							125					

ANSWER SHEET

SEP 2013

TEST NO. _____ PART _____ TITLE OF POSITION _____

(AS GIVEN IN EXAMINATION ANNOUNCEMENT - INCLUDE OPTION, IF ANY)

PLACE OF EXAMINATION _____ DATE ____

(CITY OR TOWN)   (STATE)

RATING

USE THE SPECIAL PENCIL. MAKE GLOSSY BLACK MARKS.

	A B C D E		A B C D E		A B C D E		A B C D E		A B C D E
1	⋮ ⋮ ⋮ ⋮ ⋮	26	⋮ ⋮ ⋮ ⋮ ⋮	51	⋮ ⋮ ⋮ ⋮ ⋮	76	⋮ ⋮ ⋮ ⋮ ⋮	101	⋮ ⋮ ⋮ ⋮ ⋮
2	⋮ ⋮ ⋮ ⋮ ⋮	27	⋮ ⋮ ⋮ ⋮ ⋮	52	⋮ ⋮ ⋮ ⋮ ⋮	77	⋮ ⋮ ⋮ ⋮ ⋮	102	⋮ ⋮ ⋮ ⋮ ⋮
3	⋮ ⋮ ⋮ ⋮ ⋮	28	⋮ ⋮ ⋮ ⋮ ⋮	53	⋮ ⋮ ⋮ ⋮ ⋮	78	⋮ ⋮ ⋮ ⋮ ⋮	103	⋮ ⋮ ⋮ ⋮ ⋮
4	⋮ ⋮ ⋮ ⋮ ⋮	29	⋮ ⋮ ⋮ ⋮ ⋮	54	⋮ ⋮ ⋮ ⋮ ⋮	79	⋮ ⋮ ⋮ ⋮ ⋮	104	⋮ ⋮ ⋮ ⋮ ⋮
5	⋮ ⋮ ⋮ ⋮ ⋮	30	⋮ ⋮ ⋮ ⋮ ⋮	55	⋮ ⋮ ⋮ ⋮ ⋮	80	⋮ ⋮ ⋮ ⋮ ⋮	105	⋮ ⋮ ⋮ ⋮ ⋮
6	⋮ ⋮ ⋮ ⋮ ⋮	31	⋮ ⋮ ⋮ ⋮ ⋮	56	⋮ ⋮ ⋮ ⋮ ⋮	81	⋮ ⋮ ⋮ ⋮ ⋮	106	⋮ ⋮ ⋮ ⋮ ⋮
7	⋮ ⋮ ⋮ ⋮ ⋮	32	⋮ ⋮ ⋮ ⋮ ⋮	57	⋮ ⋮ ⋮ ⋮ ⋮	82	⋮ ⋮ ⋮ ⋮ ⋮	107	⋮ ⋮ ⋮ ⋮ ⋮
8	⋮ ⋮ ⋮ ⋮ ⋮	33	⋮ ⋮ ⋮ ⋮ ⋮	58	⋮ ⋮ ⋮ ⋮ ⋮	83	⋮ ⋮ ⋮ ⋮ ⋮	108	⋮ ⋮ ⋮ ⋮ ⋮
9	⋮ ⋮ ⋮ ⋮ ⋮	34	⋮ ⋮ ⋮ ⋮ ⋮	59	⋮ ⋮ ⋮ ⋮ ⋮	84	⋮ ⋮ ⋮ ⋮ ⋮	109	⋮ ⋮ ⋮ ⋮ ⋮
10	⋮ ⋮ ⋮ ⋮ ⋮	35	⋮ ⋮ ⋮ ⋮ ⋮	60	⋮ ⋮ ⋮ ⋮ ⋮	85	⋮ ⋮ ⋮ ⋮ ⋮	110	⋮ ⋮ ⋮ ⋮ ⋮

Make only ONE mark for each answer. Additional and stray marks may be counted as mistakes. In making corrections, erase errors COMPLETELY.

	A B C D E		A B C D E		A B C D E		A B C D E		A B C D E
11	⋮ ⋮ ⋮ ⋮ ⋮	36	⋮ ⋮ ⋮ ⋮ ⋮	61	⋮ ⋮ ⋮ ⋮ ⋮	86	⋮ ⋮ ⋮ ⋮ ⋮	111	⋮ ⋮ ⋮ ⋮ ⋮
12	⋮ ⋮ ⋮ ⋮ ⋮	37	⋮ ⋮ ⋮ ⋮ ⋮	62	⋮ ⋮ ⋮ ⋮ ⋮	87	⋮ ⋮ ⋮ ⋮ ⋮	112	⋮ ⋮ ⋮ ⋮ ⋮
13	⋮ ⋮ ⋮ ⋮ ⋮	38	⋮ ⋮ ⋮ ⋮ ⋮	63	⋮ ⋮ ⋮ ⋮ ⋮	88	⋮ ⋮ ⋮ ⋮ ⋮	113	⋮ ⋮ ⋮ ⋮ ⋮
14	⋮ ⋮ ⋮ ⋮ ⋮	39	⋮ ⋮ ⋮ ⋮ ⋮	64	⋮ ⋮ ⋮ ⋮ ⋮	89	⋮ ⋮ ⋮ ⋮ ⋮	114	⋮ ⋮ ⋮ ⋮ ⋮
15	⋮ ⋮ ⋮ ⋮ ⋮	40	⋮ ⋮ ⋮ ⋮ ⋮	65	⋮ ⋮ ⋮ ⋮ ⋮	90	⋮ ⋮ ⋮ ⋮ ⋮	115	⋮ ⋮ ⋮ ⋮ ⋮
16	⋮ ⋮ ⋮ ⋮ ⋮	41	⋮ ⋮ ⋮ ⋮ ⋮	66	⋮ ⋮ ⋮ ⋮ ⋮	91	⋮ ⋮ ⋮ ⋮ ⋮	116	⋮ ⋮ ⋮ ⋮ ⋮
17	⋮ ⋮ ⋮ ⋮ ⋮	42	⋮ ⋮ ⋮ ⋮ ⋮	67	⋮ ⋮ ⋮ ⋮ ⋮	92	⋮ ⋮ ⋮ ⋮ ⋮	117	⋮ ⋮ ⋮ ⋮ ⋮
18	⋮ ⋮ ⋮ ⋮ ⋮	43	⋮ ⋮ ⋮ ⋮ ⋮	68	⋮ ⋮ ⋮ ⋮ ⋮	93	⋮ ⋮ ⋮ ⋮ ⋮	118	⋮ ⋮ ⋮ ⋮ ⋮
19	⋮ ⋮ ⋮ ⋮ ⋮	44	⋮ ⋮ ⋮ ⋮ ⋮	69	⋮ ⋮ ⋮ ⋮ ⋮	94	⋮ ⋮ ⋮ ⋮ ⋮	119	⋮ ⋮ ⋮ ⋮ ⋮
20	⋮ ⋮ ⋮ ⋮ ⋮	45	⋮ ⋮ ⋮ ⋮ ⋮	70	⋮ ⋮ ⋮ ⋮ ⋮	95	⋮ ⋮ ⋮ ⋮ ⋮	120	⋮ ⋮ ⋮ ⋮ ⋮
21	⋮ ⋮ ⋮ ⋮ ⋮	46	⋮ ⋮ ⋮ ⋮ ⋮	71	⋮ ⋮ ⋮ ⋮ ⋮	96	⋮ ⋮ ⋮ ⋮ ⋮	121	⋮ ⋮ ⋮ ⋮ ⋮
22	⋮ ⋮ ⋮ ⋮ ⋮	47	⋮ ⋮ ⋮ ⋮ ⋮	72	⋮ ⋮ ⋮ ⋮ ⋮	97	⋮ ⋮ ⋮ ⋮ ⋮	122	⋮ ⋮ ⋮ ⋮ ⋮
23	⋮ ⋮ ⋮ ⋮ ⋮	48	⋮ ⋮ ⋮ ⋮ ⋮	73	⋮ ⋮ ⋮ ⋮ ⋮	98	⋮ ⋮ ⋮ ⋮ ⋮	123	⋮ ⋮ ⋮ ⋮ ⋮
24	⋮ ⋮ ⋮ ⋮ ⋮	49	⋮ ⋮ ⋮ ⋮ ⋮	74	⋮ ⋮ ⋮ ⋮ ⋮	99	⋮ ⋮ ⋮ ⋮ ⋮	124	⋮ ⋮ ⋮ ⋮ ⋮
25	⋮ ⋮ ⋮ ⋮ ⋮	50	⋮ ⋮ ⋮ ⋮ ⋮	75	⋮ ⋮ ⋮ ⋮ ⋮	100	⋮ ⋮ ⋮ ⋮ ⋮	125	⋮ ⋮ ⋮ ⋮ ⋮